Come With Me

A
SUGARLAND CREEK
PREQUEL

BROOKE MONTGOMERY

Playlist

Listen to the *Come With Me* playlist on Spotify

Greatest Love Story | LANCO
when was it over? | Sasha Alex Sloan, Sam Hunt
More Than My Hometown | Morgan Wallen
I Want You Back | Taylor Swift
Wait | Maroon 5
One | Ed Sheeran
Just Give Me a Reason | P!nk, Nate Ruess
If You're Not The One | Daniel Bedingfield
Whatever It Takes | Lifehouse
Back To You | Selena
Never Really Over | Katy Perry
Let's Be Us Again | Lonestar
Here Without You | 3 Doors Down
The Man I Want to Be | Chris Young
Unforgettable | Thomas Rhett
Tennessee Whiskey | Chris Stapleton
Die From A Broken Heart | Maddie & Tae

Welcome to

SUGARLAND CREEK

RANCH AND EQUINE RETREAT

SUGARLAND CREEK, TN

~Welcome to Sugarland Creek Ranch and Equine Retreat~

The town of Sugarland Creek is home to over two thousand residents and is surrounded by the beautiful Appalachian Mountains. We're only fifteen minutes from the downtown area, where you can shop at local boutiques, grab a latte, catch a movie, or simply enjoy the views.

We're an all-inclusive ranch. While we provide rustic lodging, each cabin is handicapped-accessible with ramps and smooth walking trails. If you need assistance with traveling between activities, we'll provide you with a staff member to pick you up in one of our handicapped-accessible vehicles at any time. Please request at the front desk or dial '0' on your room phone. We're here to help in any way we can.

To make your stay here the best experience, meet the family and learn about everything we have to offer at the retreat to ensure you have the vacation of a lifetime!

Meet the Hollis family:

Garrett & Dena Hollis

Mr. and Mrs. Hollis have been married for over thirty years and have five children. The Sugarland Creek Ranch has been home to over three Hollis generations. When the family officially took over twenty years ago, they added on the retreat to share their love of horses and the outdoors with the public.

Wilder and Waylon
Twin boys, the oldest

Landen
The middle child

Tripp
Youngest of the boys

Noah
The only girl and baby of the family

Whether you're here to relax and enjoy the views or you're ready to get your hands dirty, we have a variety of activities on the ranch for you to enjoy:

Horseback trail riding & tours
(10:00 a.m. and 4:00 p.m.)
Hiking, mountain biking, & fishing
(Maps available at The Lodge)
Family Game Nights
(Sundays and Wednesdays)
Karaoke & Square Dancing
(Friday and Saturday nights)
Kids Game Room
(Open 24/7)
Swimming
(Pool open 9:00 a.m. to 9:00 p.m. each day)
Bonfires with s'mores
(Fridays)
…and much more depending on the season!

The Lodge building is staffed 24 hours a day. It's home to our reception & guest services, The Sugarland Restaurant & Saloon, and activities sign-up.

Find all of our current information at sugarlandcreekranch.com.

We pride ourselves on serving authentic Southern food, so please let us know if you have any dietary restrictions or needs to better serve you. We offer brunch from 8:00 a.m. to 1:00 p.m. The restaurant is open for dinner from 5:00 p.m. to 9:00 p.m. If you wish to dine or find other activities off the ranch, we're less than an hour from Gatlinburg and are happy to provide you with suggestions.

Thank you so much for visiting us.
We hope you have the best time!

-The Hollis Family & Team Sugarland

See map on the next page!

B
F
A
G
EQUINE RETREAT ENTRANCE
SUGARLAND CREEK RANCH
HORSE TRAIL RIDING

(A) The Lodge/ Guest Services	(D) Pool House & Swimming Area
(B) Ranch Hand Quarters	(E) Trail Horse Barn & Pasture
(C) Guest Cabins	(F) Riding Horse Corral

SUGARLAND CREEK

RANCH AND EQUINE RETREAT

SUGARLAND CREEK, TN

Prologue
Ayden

TEN YEARS AGO

"Please, Laney. Come with me," I beg for the hundredth time.

"Don't go. Not yet. *Please*." Pleading green eyes look at me before I toss my suitcase in the back seat of my pickup and shut the door. "Ayden, you know I can't."

We've had this talk several times. She knows why I'm leaving.

"And you know why I can't be *here*." I palm her splotchy cheeks and wipe away her tears.

"What about us?" she asks while trying to catch her breath.

"You're the love of my life, Laney. That'll never change. But if you don't come with me, it's over. I'm never returnin' to Texas."

Her sobs rip through me. Fresh tears spill down her cheeks, and it takes everything inside me not to change my mind.

I'm the reason our hearts are shattering.

"Baby, if you come with me, I'll take care of you. I promise."

We're only eighteen, but she's the woman I planned on marrying. Having my children. Starting a family together. She's always been my home when my own was destructive.

I've told her for the past year that the day after we graduate from high school, I was getting out of town—out of Beaumont. After the black eye my father gave me when I told him I wasn't going to his alma mater, I knew I couldn't be here anymore.

He wanted a football star in the family.

I want to choose my own life and escape his abuse.

"Why can't you start fresh here? Get a job and save up, then we can stay together. Please, Ayden." She grabs my wrists.

She knows why. There are no options for me here. My father would make certain of that, and I'd be stuck living with *his rules*. As a high-profile attorney and the mayor, he holds all the cards. And as his only child, I could never live up to his impossible expectations. Each time I disappointed him, he took his anger out on my body while my mother clutched her bottle of Chardonnay and looked the other way.

Just like she did when I told her what he'd done to Gabby last year.

Another reason I have to leave this place. The guilt's eating me alive.

"I love you more than anything, Lane. But you know what will happen to me if I stay here."

I'll end up like *him*.

An abusive, power-hungry, angry son of a bitch who's unfaithful and a manipulating bastard. Being anything less than his idea of perfect would ruin me and everyone I love, including Laney. Not getting an athletic scholarship at his alma mater to brag about to his uptight politician buddies cost me a week in the hospital.

Not that anyone would believe me if I told them.

According to my hospital chart, I was mugged.

"No, you won't, I promise. We can move in together and have our own family. He'll never hurt you again."

I want to believe her. I want to trust that it'd be as easy as moving out, but I know better. My father would still have access to me, and to get back at me, he'd make sure no one within a hundred-mile radius would hire me.

Bending to her mouth, I hover above it for a moment, waiting to see if she'll deny me. When she doesn't, I press my lips to hers. Neither of us breathes or moves. We stay glued to each other as if our kiss can transport us to another time, another place, another reality that isn't ours.

"I love you, and that'll never change," I whisper against her lips. "I'll call when I settle in and get a new phone."

It's only a matter of time before my father cuts me off once I'm gone. I managed to save enough money from side jobs and birthdays, but it'll only last a couple of months until I find a full-time job. Someplace far away enough where he has no influence.

Laney pulls away, her eyes bloodshot and her face red. "Why bother? If you ain't comin' back, there's no point stayin' in contact."

"Baby..." I reach out, but she takes a step back.

"No. Tearin' me apart once is enough, don't you think? I don't need a reminder when you finally end up somewhere and fall in love with someone else."

"You know that'd never happen. I'll wait for you," I promise, closing the gap between us and wrapping an arm around her waist so she can't escape. "When you're ready to leave, I'll be waitin'."

"Ayden, please." The dark edge in her tone tells me waiting would be a waste of my time. "You know I can't leave my mom and the store. She needs me. This is my life. It was supposed to be *our* lives."

I don't repeat the same words from before because I've told her so many times. She knows I won't stay and why, and now we're at a stalemate. Neither willing to change our plans even though we love each other.

Snaking my other arm around her, I pull her in for a final hug. I squeeze, inhaling the scent of her shampoo and imprinting it into my memory.

Laney's shoulders tense as she leans into me but allows me this final goodbye.

"No matter what happens, remember what I said. You're the love of my life, and that'll never change. If I need to wait a decade for you, I will."

She continues to weep, soaking my shirt in the process, but I don't care. I hold her, enveloping her with my warmth as the sun sets in the distance.

"Just go." She pulls back, quickly wiping her eyes. "I have to go home and help with dinner."

We've been in my driveway for nearly an hour, and if I don't leave soon, I'll run into my father. I got rid of my luxury SUV this morning and bought a used Ford pickup truck. The type of vehicle I actually wanted, not the flashy, expensive one my father bought for appearances. I wouldn't put it past him to report my vehicle missing or have a GPS tracker on it, so the sooner I got rid of it, the better. Now he'll have no way to hunt me down.

"I'll text so you know I'm okay," I reassure her and kiss the top of her head once more. "Please be safe."

"I should be sayin' that to you," she murmurs, rubbing her eyes.

"If my dad contacts you, tell him you don't know anything,

then demand he leaves you alone," I tell her, then open the driver's side door. Bryant Carson is a monster behind closed doors, but to the public, he's a saint. Still, I wouldn't put it past him to corner Laney to get information on my whereabouts.

"Not like I'll have *any* information."

I've purposely been vague so she'd have nothing to tell him. Though I don't have anything set in stone, I've been doing my research, so I have a general idea of where I'm headed first.

I settle into my seat.

"I love you," I mouth once more.

The image of Laney with tearstained cheeks and sad eyes will forever be ingrained into my mind. She's never looked so hopeless.

It breaks my fucking heart.

I can barely breathe when she walks to her car across the round driveway. My throat constricts and my hands sweat as I fight the urge to chase after her. Laney's run-down beater chokes for a few seconds before roaring to life. She turned down my offer to buy her something more reliable since she couldn't pay it back. Not that I expected her to, but she's got her mother's pride. Ms. Bennett has been a single mom and the sole provider for Laney since she was only two.

"Get your battery checked," I shout.

She rolls down her window. "What?"

"Go to Adams and tell him to check your battery. Might be the starter, though."

He'll barely charge her for it.

It's what he called the *family and friends* discount.

"Fine." She shrugs as if she's lost the ability to care about anything.

Howie Adams has been my best friend since kindergarten and is the only other person who knows about my plans to ditch

5

this place. I said my goodbyes to him this morning when he hooked me up with a seller for my SUV. His dad owns a garage in town, and Howie's been working with him since he was thirteen.

She rolls up her window, but before she can drive away, I honk my horn three times.

I. Love. You.

It's been our thing since we could drive.

I wait, hopeful she'll do it too.

As I watch her struggle with deciding, I honk three times again, each one a little longer this time.

I.

Love.

You.

Finally, she faces me, then honks three times.

We stare at each other, both lost in the moment, both wishing this weren't goodbye.

Then she drives away.

Making sure I'm gone before my father returns from a long day of screwing his secretaries, I bolt out of the driveway, too.

Glancing in the rearview mirror, I look at the house with more bad memories than good and say goodbye to eighteen years of pain.

Half of those years were spent loving *her*, and still, our love wasn't enough to stay.

Chapter One
Ayden

PRESENT DAY

"*Taylor Alison Swift*," Mallory singsongs, skipping into the stables in her pink cowboy boots. At only eleven years old, she's the youngest in the Hollis family and *not* coincidentally, the loudest. I shouldn't even be surprised she's an obsessed Taylor Swift fan who named her quarter horse after the singer since she was born and raised in Tennessee.

"She's in the pasture," I tell her when she looks over the gate. "Her stall needs to be cleaned."

"Can you saddle her for me?" she pleads, folding her hands into a praying gesture.

"I'm busy, Mal." I make a show of holding up two large buckets of feed. "Ask Noah."

"Where is she?"

"Trainin'." *Where else?* Noah's as passionate about horse training as Mallory is about Taylor Swift.

As soon as the word leaves my lips, Mallory bolts out the

way she came in. Blond hair flies through the wind as she belts out the lyrics to "Love Story."

I shake my head with a grin. Mallory moved to the ranch a year ago after her parents died in a car crash, and the Hollises became her guardians. At the time, I'd been working here for nine years, and I'd never seen Mr. Hollis cry until the day of his wife's sister and brother-in-law's funerals. It was devastating for everyone, but especially for their only child. Mallory's gone through a lot in her short life, but ever since learning to ride here at the ranch, she's been back to her happy, free-spirited self.

It also helps that there's never a dull moment at the Sugarland Creek Ranch, which keeps her busy. The Hollises are a big family who shower her with plenty of love.

Once I finish feeding the horses, Noah walks in with Foster, the horse she's training, and Mallory skips behind them. Noah shoots me a glare, and I hold back a chuckle at the annoyed expression on her face. She grabs a lead rope, hands it to Mallory, and then tells her to bring in the horse so they can saddle her for a ride in the corral. In the meantime, she puts Foster back in his stall.

Mallory isn't experienced enough to put one on by herself, so she's required to ask an adult for help. We usually don't mind, but we're short two ranch hands this week, and since it's early June, we're at the start of our busy season with guests and boarders.

"Where are the others?" Noah asks as she hauls a saddle from the tack room.

"Trey's in Georgia for a family wedding, and Ruby is on some romantic getaway with her boyfriend to celebrate their six-monthiversary."

She stops walking and stares at me.

"Her words, not mine," I clarify.

"Who approved her vacation time for *that*?"

"Take a guess." I laugh.

"Of course. My father, right?"

"Yep."

Noah shakes her head. She's like me—all work and hardly any play.

If I've learned one thing about Garrett Hollis, he's a hopeless romantic. During the first week of my training, he talked nonstop about meeting Dena and falling madly in love the moment he laid eyes on her. They were engaged and married within three months of meeting.

"Maybe you should take a week off and go find your *Mr. Right*," I tease, grabbing a shovel and taking a wheelbarrow to Miss Swift's stall.

"If I'm takin' a week off to do anything, it's to be alone with my rose vibrator in a whirlpool tub and drinkin' expensive wine."

I grunt at the unwanted visual. "One of those things I didn't need to know."

"Hey, when you find something that snatches your soul, you'd be open about it too."

"What's a vibrator?" Mallory asks. She has her horse next to her, waiting.

Noah's face pales as she quickly spins around. "Um, nothin'. It's like a back massager."

"Cool! Can I get one?"

"No!" Noah blurts out, grabbing the saddle pad and placing it on the horse's back. "It's for adults only."

Mallory frowns. "That's not fair. I'm gonna ask Uncle Garrett. He'll buy one for me."

Noah turns and scowls at me for not warning her Mallory

was behind her. Laughing, I continue shoveling and keep my mouth closed.

"You wanna learn to do this on your own someday, then I reckon you pay attention," Noah scolds when Mallory continues rambling about getting a vibrator.

"Yes, ma'am."

As soon as Miss Swift is brushed, saddled, and Mallory's situated on top, Noah leads them out to the corral, and I finish up her stall.

"How are things goin'?" Waylon asks, mud covering his face and soaking through his clothes.

"What the hell happened to you?"

"Four-wheeler got stuck, so I pushed from behind while Wilder steered, and well, ya see how that turned out."

I chuckle. "Damn, wish I'd witnessed that."

Wilder comes strolling in with a shit-eating grin on his face. He's as clean as a whistle.

They're identical twins, but their personalities couldn't be more different. They're the oldest of the Hollis kids but not necessarily the maturest.

"Not sure that's only mud," Wilder taunts.

"It better be or—" Waylon sprints toward his brother and tackles him to the ground.

"Dude, what the fuck?" Wilder fights back, and unless there's blood, I don't get involved.

Wilder's known as the rowdy twin for a reason, and even if he doesn't start the fights, he's sure to finish them.

"Hey!" Noah shouts, rushing back in. "What in the Sam Hill are y'all doin'? We have guests here!"

You'd think this would cause a scene, but it's a common occurrence. The twins messing around, and their little sister telling them to get their shit together.

"Quit pitchin' a fit. All the guests checked out, and the new ones haven't arrived yet," Wilder tells her.

"I don't care," Noah snaps. "Hush your mouths and grow up."

"You first," he shoots back.

Noah rolls her eyes as she takes the shovel from my hand and threatens to flatten them to the concrete.

"Who licked the red off your candy?" Wilder growls.

Waylon laughs, and if they keep pushing her buttons, I'll let her do as she promised.

"Go be useful. We're short-staffed as it is. Help Ayden finish up in here."

"Nah, don't stick me with the twins. I got this," I blurt out, taking the shovel from her death grip.

"I gotta get back to Mallory, so make sure they get to work," she tells me before storming off.

You'd think a bunch of teenagers were managing the ranch, but the twins are only a year younger than me. Noah's the youngest of the Hollis siblings and handles them like she's their mother. It's quite comical. Took me a bit to get used to the dynamic, but the Hollises became the family I wished I'd had.

"The goats need to be moved to the other pasture. Think one of you can manage that?" I ask, heading to the next stall.

"Wilder will do it," Waylon offers for his brother. "While I go shower."

Just as the twins are having a stare off, another Hollis sibling enters on a dirt bike.

"We havin' a family meetin' or something?" Landen asks. He looks nothing like the twins and is the middle child but acts the most like Wilder out of the brothers. Both are rowdy playboys who never take life seriously.

"Get that outta here. You know it spooks the horses." I

wave Landen away. As the breeding operations manager, he knows the rules.

"I was just comin' to help. Noah texted."

Jesus Christ. "I'm *fine*. If y'all would get the hell out and stop slowin' me down, I wouldn't need help."

Wilder shrugs. "'Kay, fine. I'm off like a herd of turtles."

He tends to the goats while Waylon goes to clean up, and Landen takes the trailer to the barn to unload hay into the loft. With the three of them out of my hair, I get back to shoveling shit so I can bring the horses back in.

An hour later, the stalls are cleaned out with fresh feed and water. When my phone rings, I see Tripp's name.

"Yes?" I answer.

"I need someone for cabin call."

"That ain't my job."

I walk to the back of the barn where my office and the restrooms are located. As the boarding operations manager, I oversee the stables, not the trail horses.

"Waylon ain't answering, and six new guests signed up for the four o'clock riding session."

I sigh. "Fine."

Each person who stays in the cabins at the equine retreat and wants to go trail riding must use the same horse during their stay. The Hollises wanted a curated experience for each guest and based on their riding knowledge and age, we select which horse we provide for them. It's Tripp's job to oversee check-ins and tell Waylon which ones need to be saddled and ready for the afternoon tour.

"Go ahead," I say once I grab a notepad and pen.

The twins manage the trail ride tours, which are twice a day, once in the morning and once in the afternoon. They're usually good about being on time, but with them, you never know.

"Got it." I'm ready to hang up and hunt down Waylon.

"Also, someone's here for ya." He hesitates before continuing. "A woman."

"Who?"

"Not sure. She asked if you were workin' today, and I said I'd see about findin' ya. She's a looker, too."

Scoffing, I say, "Alright, I'll be there shortly."

I end the call and take the piece of paper with me as I walk out of the barn.

Noah's in the corral with one of the boarders, but Mallory's nowhere to be found. I was hoping she saw them. Though she's just a kid, she's a little gossip queen who keeps tabs on everyone.

Grabbing my phone, I click on Waylon's name.

He picks up. "What?"

"You missed cabin call. I got the list."

"Shit. Be right there."

We end the call, and I turn to Noah. "How's Brighton doin'?"

"She's feisty today." Noah clicks her tongue, trying to get her to move a certain way. Noah's a natural-born horse expert. Even at eleven years old when I first met her, I could tell she had a special gift. She gets paid the big bucks for training show horses. I don't think Noah's taken more than a day off a week in the past five years. She's already booked out for the next two with clients who want her to train their horses for competitions, barrel racing, and jumping.

"She's scheduled to leave in a couple weeks. Think she'll be ready?" I ask.

"Oh yeah. She's bound to have an off day, but she'll be good to go. Plus, we'll need her stall for the next one."

"I'm sure Tripp could come down this evenin' if you need

assistance," I suggest as I wait for Waylon to hurry his ass down here.

Tripp's only two years older than her and is an experienced trainer, too. He pitches in when Noah needs a hand, but I know her well enough to know she's too prideful to admit when she needs help.

"He's already workin' on Rosebud and Jewels. Plus, he's on guest services this weekend," she says as she continues Brighton's lunges.

Friday and Saturday nights are karaoke and square dancing nights for the guests. We all take turns emceeing since it's the least desired job at the retreat. Well, except for Wilder, who enjoys the attention. Ever since a video of him went viral a year ago, he's requested almost every weekend. A bunch of thirsty housewives couldn't get enough of his flirty antics and always want more of him shaking his ass. He might as well. He makes the most tips out of all of us.

"Right, but I'm sure if you—"

"You losin' faith in me, Ayden?" she teases.

"Never. You're amazin', you know that. Just worry about ya. Like an annoyin' little sister who never takes a moment for herself."

"I take offense to that."

"You know I'm kiddin'." I chuckle. "What would I do without your entertainin' last-minute mania to make your deadlines?"

She snorts. "Have a life of your own, maybe?"

Though each day can be chaotic, I'm grateful for it. My mind stays busy, and not knowing what to expect each morning keeps things interesting and fun most of the time.

Finally, Waylon arrives in his pickup. "Sorry, I left my

phone in my truck when I went to shower, and then Ma distracted me with food."

I hand him the list. "Better be quick. They all want on the afternoon tour."

He grunts. "Yeah, yeah."

"I gotta run to The Lodge. Have fun." I smack his shoulder as I walk around him and hop into my truck.

As I drive past the stables and pastures, I reflect on my first day here. I'd hoped Garrett would take pity on me and give me a job. I was willing to do anything. Work any shift and any number of hours. He said considering I was coming with no experience and being only eighteen, he'd give me *one* chance to prove myself. No fucking up, no showing up late, and no costly mistakes.

By the end of my shift, I was so goddamn sore I could barely walk the next day. But I was determined to earn this job.

The most laborious job I'd had up until then was cleaning pools for the country club wives. You'd think four years of high school football would've prepared me, but it hadn't. The longest I played for was a few hours. My first day on the ranch lasted twelve.

But I didn't give up because I had something to prove—to myself—and I wasn't about to be a quitter. Especially after what it took for me to leave and the people there who meant everything to me.

When I pull into the parking lot, I quickly find a spot. Since cabins stay booked year-round, it's always busy on this side of the property. The Hollises have a full staff to help the retreat run smoothly and over a dozen ranch hands to keep up with the horses and maintenance.

The boarding and training side of the ranch is much calmer,

but we stay just as busy keeping up with the stables and training.

When I walk through the doors, I see Tripp behind the front desk as if he's been waiting for me. The guests are checked in by the looks of the empty waiting room, but the receptionist is busy on the phone.

"Hey, man." I walk up to the counter.

"Over there." He nods in the direction of someone behind me. The smirk planted on his face is uneasy as if he's keeping a secret.

When I turn around, she stands from a chair.

All the air vanishes from my lungs.

It can't be. There's no way she's in front of me right now, yet she is.

Long golden blond hair swims around her shoulders as sparkling green eyes stare into mine.

She steps toward me, but I'm too shocked to move.

Laney Bennett.

"Hi, Ayden," she finally speaks, soft and gentle as she fidgets with her fingers.

"You can't be here, Laney." My voice comes out much harsher than I mean to, but I can't help the fear of my father lingering somewhere in the bushes. It's pathetic that I'm still scared of him after all this time, but it's instinctual after putting up with his abuse for eighteen years. He'd probably laugh in my face if he knew that fear of him still haunts me. I'm no longer a child, and I shouldn't let it bury me alive.

Her face etches in pain, and the guilt hits me as soon as it flashes across her pretty features.

"Sorry, I shouldn't have said that." I lift my ball cap and scrub a hand through my hair as I step closer. "I'm shocked to see you, is all. How are you? How'd you find me?"

Laney looks behind me. "Is there somewhere quiet we can go?"

Glancing over my shoulder, I notice Tripp watching us. *Nosy bastard.*

"Yeah, of course. My truck's out front. Come with me." Out of habit, I grab her hand, and when she doesn't pull away, I link my fingers between hers. They're just as warm and inviting as I remember.

"You still have that old thing?" she asks as I lead her outside.

Chuckling, I sneak another glance. "Of course. Good ole Betty Lou hasn't let me down yet."

She laughs, and the sound of it feels like home.

I open the passenger side door, help her in, and then round the front and jump into the driver's side. "I live in the ranch hand quarters if you don't mind going there? It'll be private."

"Fine with me."

Once we're out of the parking lot, I look over and admire how beautiful she still looks. Laney's always been drop-dead gorgeous, but she's matured over the past decade. Fuller lips, thicker hair, rounder hips. *Absolutely stunning.*

"I saw a video of you," she begins, and my heart races.

"How? What was I doing?"

She must hear the panic in my tone because she leans over and squeezes my thigh. "He doesn't know where you are, Ayden. It's okay."

I nod, appreciating that she understands.

"Someone posted a video from their bachelorette party. They were just a bunch of clips, but in one of them, you were standin' next to a horse with a devilish smirk on your face. One of the women asked if they could ride the cowboy instead of the horse."

I snort, laughing at the memory. "Ah, yes. I remember that. I was coverin' for Wilder, who called in sick that day. Wait. That party was from three months ago."

"Yeah."

"It took you that long to find the ranch?"

"Oh." She pulls her hand back into her lap and looks down. "No, it was easy to find the location since they tagged it, but I wasn't sure if I should just show up. I also couldn't take off work right away. I had to make arrangements. And also, find the courage."

I pull up in front of my house and park, then turn and face her. "So what made you come now?"

She swallows hard as she avoids eye contact, and I can tell something's wrong.

"Laney, what is it?"

Finally, she lifts her head and frowns. "Howie died."

Chapter Two
Laney

Ayden's breath gets caught in his throat as soon as I release those two words.

Howie died.

He deserved to know. I didn't want to send him a letter with the news. I needed to see him in person because I had so much to say.

Needed to make sure he was okay after all this time.

I spent years looking for him. He sent me a letter six weeks after he left to tell me he was somewhere safe and working, but didn't leave a return address or a phone number. It was a painful reminder that we were over. There'd never be a way for me to find him unless he wanted me to. The guilt of telling him not to bother keeping in contact because I was hurting has gnawed at me since the day he left. If I'd told him to write or call me, he would've, but I figured the sooner we cut off contact, the less it'd hurt.

"How?" he chokes out.

"Car crash. He was passin' a tractor, and a semi turned

down the road. They say he probably didn't see the semi until it was too late, and they had nowhere to go except into each other."

"Jesus." He shakes his head, disbelief washing over his features. "When?"

"Last Wednesday. His funeral's in three days."

"Fuck." He slams his fist into the steering wheel, making the horn blast, and I nearly jump out of my skin. "I'm sorry. I just..."

"It's okay. The town's reaction's been the same." *Especially mine.*

He frowns, and it breaks my heart to see him this upset and sad. "I thought maybe I'd get to see him again, *eventually*."

"He did, too," I admit.

"Let's go inside. I'll get you something to drink."

Howie's death wasn't all I needed to tell him, but his head was spinning with this news, so the rest would wait.

Ayden exits without waiting for a response. I hop out of the truck and meet him on the sidewalk.

"Wow, these are nice cabins." I look around and notice there are four identical ones. "How many people live here?"

"Each floor has two bedrooms. The Hollises—the family I work for—their twins share the duplex beside me. Two guys live above me, but I don't have a roommate. The other two cabins are full with four ranch hands in each."

"You get yours to yourself. I bet that's nice," I say as I unlock the front door.

"It is, but most of us aren't around much. We work twelve-plus-hour days and then usually have a beer or two at night before we crash and do it again the next day."

Once we're inside, he flicks on some lights, and I notice how empty it is. No decorations or photos. It looks vacant.

"Sweet tea?" he asks, heading toward the kitchen.

"Sure, thanks." I continue looking around.

Once he hands me a glass, I take a sip. "Love what you've done with the place."

He chuckles. "Yeah, like I said, I'm not home much. When I am, it's to shower, eat, and sleep."

Ayden stands across from me as I sit on the stool at the small breakfast bar. It's surreal to see him again after all this time. He's bigger, but his boyish face is the same.

"Are you happy here?" I ask hesitantly, and though I want to ask him a million questions, I don't want to overwhelm him or make things awkward.

"I'm not *unhappy*. I love my job and feel like I have a purpose. The room and board are cheap. Mrs. Hollis invites me to their big family dinner every Sunday, which is nice, considerin' mine were always so uncomfortable."

Yeah, I remember.

His parents had a talent for making him feel unwanted, and I hated that for him. His father then took it out on me.

"I looked up everything I could find about the ranch before deciding to come. The pictures are beautiful."

If I was being completely honest, I spent the past three months obsessing over it. Looking up the ranch's hashtags and seeing if there were any new videos or pictures of him.

"Are you stayin' a while? I could show you 'round and give you the proper tour." He leans on the counter, inches from me.

"Just one night. I booked a room in town. I wasn't sure what your reaction would be to me comin', so I didn't want to overstay my welcome. Plus, I have to get back for Howie's funeral," I admit, my heart squeezing as I think about the secrets I'll have to share.

"I wish I could go, Laney, but we're already short-staffed at the ranch. Not to mention, I wouldn't want anyone to know I was in town," he says, his piercing brown eyes gazing into mine. He means he wouldn't want his *father* to find out. The man who's ruined not only his life but tried to ruin mine, too.

"I know." I nod. "I wish I'd come sooner so that maybe Howie could've come too, but when he died, I knew I had to tell you in person. In a way, it was the push I needed to face you."

"I'm happy you did."

"You are?"

"Not about the circumstances, no. Seeing you again, yes." He smiles wide. "Were you two close? Did you stay friends?"

Nodding, I take a nervous drink. "Yeah."

"How's his dad takin' it?"

"Not great. He's a wreck. I'd been helpin' him and his grandmother plan as much of the service as I could, but they're still in shock."

"*Fuck.* I can't imagine. Did the other driver survive?"

"He's in critical condition with a brain injury. They say Howie died on impact and probably felt no pain. It's helped us cope a little."

He nods again, and we finish our sweet tea in silence.

"Let me show you 'round. I'll introduce you to Noah. She's either at the stables or trainin' center, and her brothers should be around, too," he says, setting our empty glasses in the sink.

"She's the show horse trainer, right? I read about her on the website."

And saw her model-worthy photos.

Ayden rubs a hand through his hair before replacing his hat. He never used to wear ball caps, but I like how it looks on him.

"Yep, that's her. She's a hard-ass when it comes to business

24

but very nice and bubbly when she isn't stressed. We work in the stables together."

"She looked young in her picture."

"She is. Twenty-one. Her brothers got her loaded on her birthday a few months ago. The only time I've seen her drink. I think she got sick enough to last her a lifetime." He chuckles.

I smile, remembering how I spent my twenty-first birthday.

At home, rocking my toddler to sleep and then folding laundry.

Noah might be young, but by the sounds of it, they spend a lot of time together. I try not to think of the women he's been with in the past decade, but it's hard not to be jealous. He left me behind and the future we planned. I've accepted that, even if it hasn't been easy.

Ayden places our glasses in the sink. "I'm gonna change into some nicer jeans and a different shirt. Be right back."

Five minutes later, he returns, and I visibly wipe the drool off my chin. It's not fair for him to look this good. Working on a ranch has done his body *good*. His dark jeans and white T-shirt combo shouldn't be so hot, but now he's paired it with a beanie. I have to pick up my jaw off the floor. That I do remember him wearing in high school, and it's no wonder I was so attracted to him. He fills out his shirt more now, but everything else about him is the same. Brown hair, brown eyes, and irresistible dimples.

"Ready? We'll stop at the stables first."

I clear my throat, which turned dry when he walked in here, and quickly nod. "Yep."

The view is to die for. Mountains and miles of fields line the horizon.

"This part of the ranch is on the southwest side where we

board horses and all the trainin' happens. I oversee the boardin' and do ranch hand duties."

"What's that entail?"

"Eh, bitch work mostly. Cleaning stalls, loadin' hay, callin' clients, and keeping track of each horse's needs. Whatever needs to get done, I'll do. Unloading pallets of feed, fillin' water buckets, groomin'. Noah stays busy with the trainin', so I try to do all the basic necessities so she can focus on that."

"So she trains all of them?"

"Just the show horses. The others are boarders who we take care of but don't compete. She takes them out to do lunges and get exercise, but that's it. She and her brother, Tripp, do the trainin', but Noah takes on more than he does because she's crazy like that. They're only here for a specific length of time to get them ready for competitions. The others stay here year-round because their owners live in town, but they still want to ride, so they need a place to keep them. Most have been here for years, so when the vet and farrier come, it's my job to make sure they stay updated on their vaccines and keep track of which ones need their hooves cleaned or shoed. The Hollises have their own personal horses too, but they stay in a barn closer to the main house. The parents and siblings take turns managin' them."

"Sounds like y'all have a smooth system."

He laughs. "Yeah, most days."

After we park and get out, I follow him to the barn. It's much larger than I expected. There have to be a couple of dozen stalls inside.

"Wow, there's so many. You remember all their names?"

"Yep. Like housing little toddlers and memorizin' all their likes and dislikes."

I swallow hard at the metaphor.

"Noah?" Ayden calls out. "You around?"

My heart hammers when she pops her head out from one of the stalls. "In here."

She's even more gorgeous in person.

When we reach her, I notice she's brushing a horse and rubbing soft circles along its forehead.

"I want ya to meet someone. This is Laney."

Noah's eyes widen with a grin. "*The* Laney?"

"Shut up. It's just Laney."

My brain squeals at the thought of Ayden talking about me.

"It's nice to meet you," I say, holding out my hand but then realizing how stupid I look when her hands are full.

"Likewise!" She comes closer anyway and shakes it. "Sorry, I'm sweatin' like a sinner in church. I didn't know Ayden was bringing a visitor."

"I surprised him. He didn't know," I clarify.

"Oh, how sweet."

"I'm gonna show her 'round and give her the *unfiltered* tour of the ranch. Think you can cover for me for a bit?" Ayden asks.

"Yeah, sure. But you owe me!"

"Add it to my tab," Ayden taunts.

It's then I realize their relationship isn't a romantic one. It's more of a sibling one. Relief washes over me even though I have no reason to feel an ounce of hope. It's clear he'll never return to Texas. He's found a family here.

Ayden takes my hand and leads us down the walkway, talking about a few of his favorite horses and the inside of the tack room. Then we walk into a back room makeshift office, but I can hardly focus with his strong hand enveloping mine.

"It's not much, but it's where I make the boardin' schedules and speak to clients. I also keep track of expenses and payments."

"It has more personality than your entire house," I tease. "At least there's pictures on the walls."

Most are newspaper clippings and horse photos.

"To be fair, I'm here more than at home." He shrugs.

Next, we walk out to the pasture. "Is that a goat?"

"That one's Shelly Belly. Careful, she's an old, sassy one."

I step back. "They just roam free?"

"Kinda, but she's an escape artist. The rules don't apply to her," he explains with a shrug.

"What do they do?"

"Graze mostly. Eat up the brush and wild vegetation. It helps control the shrubs. We move them from pasture to pasture."

When we walk the fence line, one of the horses approaches. "This is Mayberry. She's a show horse with a strict schedule of eatin', exercisin', and jumpin'. Noah works with her every day."

She nuzzles her nose against his hand.

"I'm surprised she's allowed to be out here," I say, remembering what little knowledge I have. The risk of injury is higher when they're frolicking in a pasture.

"Yeah, it's why she's out here alone and only for a short time after trainin'."

"I bet you've learned a lot workin' here," I say as we walk back toward the barn.

He chuckles. "More than I could've ever wanted to know. Now it feels like second nature."

"Ayden." I stop, hoping he'll do the same. When he faces me, I inhale. "I'm really proud of you. I know I was angry and heartbroken when you left, but it looks like you've made a good life for yourself. I'm happy you got the fresh start you wanted."

He closes the gap between us. "I'm sorry I had to start over without you. Not a day goes by that I haven't thought about you. Wonderin' how you were doing. If you were happy and safe. If a man was treatin' you right. My biggest regret in life was havin' to walk away from you."

Tears form in the corner of my eyes. I hate that I'm not strong enough to keep my emotions in check, but when it comes to Ayden—the boy I never stopped loving—his words shoot straight to my heart.

"I'm sorry, too. I wish I could've come with you. This would've been an awesome place to raise a family."

He raises his brows as if it just occurred to him to ask if I had a family.

"Are you married?"

I shake my head.

"What about kids?"

This time, I nod.

"Really?" He genuinely smiles. "How old?"

I suck in a breath because there's no avoiding this. It's part of the reason I came here.

"She's nine."

His brown eyes stay glued to mine, neither of us moving or speaking while his brain catches up.

"Who's the father?" he finally asks, his voice gruff and angry as he folds his arms across his chest.

"Ayden," I say his name calmly. "Can we not do this right now, please?" I look around in case we aren't alone.

"We're not moving until you answer my question. Who's. Her. Father?"

"Who do you think?" I shrug, then rub my sweaty palms along my jeans. "I didn't find out until after you left."

"Jesus Christ, Laney." He paces. "You could've led with that."

"I didn't want to overwhelm you. Howie's death was already big news to share."

"I have a daughter?" His voice cracks as he stops in front of me.

"*We* have a daughter, yes."

"Is she here?"

"No, she's with my mother in Texas."

"Does she know about me?"

"Howie and I talked about you a lot, yes. She doesn't know the details of why you left, but she knows you exist—somewhere."

"I can't fuckin' believe this. *Shit*." He shakes his head in disbelief and then grabs my hand. "I would've never left, Laney. I swear, I would've stayed and raised our daughter with you. I would've married you. I'd—"

"I know, Ayden. I never doubted for a moment you wouldn't have been the best father. For years, I tried to find you. You were never on social media. Your phone number was disconnected. Eventually, I saved up money to hire a PI to check if you had opened any credit cards or a bank account, but he came back empty."

"You've been raisin' her by yourself?"

"No, I had help."

He frowns, releasing me. "But not mine."

"You didn't know," I remind him softly.

"What's her name?"

"Serena Mae."

He tilts his head, and those soulful brown eyes light up every nerve under my skin. "You named her after *my* grandmother?"

I can't help but smile. "I knew how much you loved her, and I loved her name. I wanted to honor you somehow."

"Wow. I don't know what to say. I don't even deserve the chance to be her dad after being away for nine years."

"*Ayden Carson*, that's not true," I scold, inching closer until I'm at eye level with his chest. He has a good six inches on me. "You had no idea. Hell, I didn't know for a month because I thought it was heartbreak sickness. It wasn't until I realized I missed my period that I finally took a test, and well...*surprise*."

He cups my cheek, and I can't stop myself from leaning into his warm palm. "God, I'm sorry. I should've put my new number in my letter so you could've at least called and told me. I would've come back in a heartbeat."

"That's partially my fault too. I told you not to."

"Can I meet her?"

"Yeah, of course."

"When?"

"I'm not sure. It's a bit complicated. I need to take off work and—"

"What if I come there?"

My brows shoot up at the sudden change of heart. "*Really*? You'd come to Beaumont?"

"To meet my daughter, yes. I can't go to the funeral, but I'd like to visit Howie's grave and pay my respects in private when I'm there."

"That'd be great, Ayden. Seriously."

He takes me by surprise and wraps me in a hug, but I don't back away. Ayden's touch is something I've been dreaming of, and just like always, it gives me comfort and hope. I inhale the scent of his cologne, and years of memories flash through my mind.

"Do you have any pictures?" he asks when we break apart.

"Yeah, thousands." I laugh just thinking about how many I've taken over the past nine years.

"Let's eat at The Lodge tonight, and you can show me. Start with when you were pregnant. I bet you were cute as hell."

I burst out laughing. "Oh my God. It'll take us a year to get through them all."

He smirks. "I've got time."

Chapter Three
Ayden

I'm still in shock about the news of Serena.

I'm a father.

I didn't see that coming.

Though at one point I dreamed of having a family with Laney, I wasn't sure if I wanted to be a dad. Considering the relationship with my parents, I wasn't sure being a good one was in my DNA.

Regardless, I can't wait to meet her and see what she's like.

If she likes the same things I did at her age.

If she looks like her mama. Or my grandmother.

Nerves surface in my stomach, and a realization that she might not like me hits home.

I didn't like my parents.

Although I'd never treat her the way mine treated me, I've already missed the first nine years of her life.

Once Laney and I sit at a table to eat, she gives me complete access to her phone's photo albums. There are *tons*.

"She looked a lot like you when she was a baby," Laney says as I scroll. "I hated it."

Chuckling, I beam at the images on the screen. Several have Howie in them too.

"There's a lot of you in her, too," I reassure.

I stare in amazement. Serena Mae has brown hair like me and emerald-green eyes like her mama.

I dig into my food and eat while Laney shares stories about each milestone and Serena's first days at school. Guilt hits me full force when I think about everything I've missed.

My brain is still spinning.

"Do you think she'll like me?" I ask when we grab dessert.

Laney nods. "She had a close relationship with Howie, and he showed her all of your yearbooks. She loved it."

"Oh God." I shake my head with laughter. "Hope he didn't let her read the messages people wrote me."

"The ones about your *tight end*?" She chuckles when my eyes widen. "He let her have them, and now she keeps them in her room. Our homecoming photo is her favorite, though she loved the ones of the parade floats, too."

King and Queen of Homecoming.

The football star and head cheerleader.

Childhood friends turned high school sweethearts.

We were the epitome of a Texas country song.

"Hard to think that was only ten years ago," I say, inching closer. Her hair falls to the side, blocking her face, and the urge to brush it back so I can stare at her rosy cheeks is almost too strong to fight.

She sighs, shifting slightly so her eyes come back into view. "Feels like yesterday and a lifetime ago all at once."

Before I have the chance to warn her, Wilder and Waylon walk up to our table. They're in their filthy work clothes and covered in dirt.

"Well, howdy." Wilder flashes a shit-eating grin, twisting his ball cap backward.

"What'd ya want?" I ask dryly, hoping they'll get the hint and go away.

"Aren't ya gonna introduce us to your *friend?*"

"Leave them alone," Waylon scolds, nudging his shoulder.

"I'm not doin' anything. He's the one who doesn't have manners. But since I'm the polite one, I'll introduce myself..."

Rolling my eyes, I wait for the *Wilder Flirt Special.*

"I'm Wilder Hollis. It's a pleasure to meet you, Miss..." He holds out his hand, smirking.

"Laney Bennett," she responds, shaking his in return.

"Wow, that's a *beautiful* name." He flashes her a wink.

"Thank you."

"I'm Waylon, the less obnoxious twin." He nods at her with his arms crossed, and she smiles in return.

"Nice to meet you," Laney replies, glancing between the twins and then me.

"Sorry," I mouth, and her face reddens.

"How do you know Ayden?" Wilder asks.

"That's none of your business," I bark, then stand from my chair. "We were just leavin'."

Laney gets to her feet and grabs our empty plates.

"Too bad." Wilder's gaze lowers down her body, and I'm tempted to remove his eye sockets so he stops eye-fucking her. "Maybe I'll see you 'round later, then."

Laney places the dishes in the tub, then I guide her toward the exit. When she's ahead, I slam my shoulder into Wilder's.

"I was just being polite," he offers.

"Well, don't," I grind out, keeping my voice low so Laney doesn't overhear.

"Wilder hates when a hot girl is off-limits to him. You just put a bounty on her." Waylon chuckles. He's well aware of his brother's antics.

We all are.

"Well, he better get used to it. Laney's leavin' soon, but either way, she's not available."

"To anyone or just me?" Wilder waggles his brows like the shit starter he is.

"*Especially* you."

I shove him out of my way once again, then meet Laney at the door.

"I take it you don't like them," she whispers.

Opening my truck door, I motion for her to get in. Then I round the front and hop in my seat.

"They're fine, but Wilder's a womanizer. He sees a woman and thinks she's a hot piece of ass for him to play with until he gets bored and moves on to the next. I had to put him in his place before he got any ideas."

She snorts, and I reverse out of my parking spot.

"What's funny?" I ask.

"Just thinkin' how nothing's changed with you."

When I get onto the main road, I glance at her. Her hair's pulled off to one shoulder, exposing her delicate neck — the one I used to cover in hickeys just to tease her.

"What do you mean?" I ask.

"You were the same way in high school."

"How so?"

"Always actin' like my big protector as if I couldn't have put that James Dean wannabe in his place."

Chuckling at her description of Wilder, I think about how she's not wrong.

"Perhaps, but he would've counted that as foreplay. Wilder is exactly what his name implies."

"And what about you?" she murmurs.

"Me what?" I pinch my brows, turning down the gravel road toward my house.

"Um, nothin'. Never mind."

"Are you tryin' to ask me if I'm *wild like Wilder*?" I ask with amusement.

She rolls her eyes, then looks out the window. "Drop it, please."

The desperation in her voice makes me wonder if she's embarrassed she asked or scared to find out, but I have no issues telling her the truth.

"Well, let's get this outta the way. I've slept with three women in the past decade," I admit, waiting to see if she'll look at me. When she doesn't, I continue. "One I dated for six months. The others were casual hookups and weren't serious."

She finally turns toward me. "When was the last one?"

"Two years ago."

Her brows lift to her hairline. "If I'm being honest, I'm surprised you're single."

"I'm not." I shrug. "You're not married, but are you seein' someone?" My heart pounds as I wait for her answer.

"I got divorced five years ago and have been single for four."

"So you dated after?"

She fidgets with her fingers in her lap, looking down at them. "Yeah, a guy I met shortly after, but it only lasted a couple months."

"Serena would've been five? How'd she take that?" I ask, pulling into my driveway and turning off the engine.

"Fine, actually. She's always been a resilient kid."

We get out and meet at the front door. Before we go inside,

I ask, "Do you wanna take a ride on the four-wheeler? We can go on a trail up the mountain and watch the sunset."

"Really? I thought maybe you'd have to get back to work or something."

"Nah, Noah's covering for me, and Tripp's doin' my night checks." I take her hand and lead us toward the nearby shed.

"Here." I grab a helmet and place it over her head, then fasten it underneath her neck. "Feel tight enough?"

She wiggles and smiles. "Yep."

After I put the other on and secure it in place, I jump on one of the ATVs. Once it's started, I nod for her to slide in behind me.

Laney plasters her chest against my back, and it's a feeling I never want to let go of. Her arms wrap around my waist, and she locks her fingers together.

"Ready?" I ask over the engine, tapping her hands.

She squeezes tighter. "Let's go, cowboy."

I laugh at the amusement in her tone and reverse out of the shed. The ride on the trail is peaceful, and the view is one I've become accustomed to. We have another hour until the sun sets, but the golden hour hue bathes the pastures in yellows, oranges, and reds like a scenic watercolor painting.

As we ride farther up, I wave to a couple hiking down and use it as an excuse to brush my hand over hers.

"Doin' okay?"

"Great." She squeezes tighter.

Less than ten minutes later, I park off the trail, and we hop off. We remove our helmets, and then I weave my fingers through hers and lead her to my favorite spot.

"Okay, almost there. I want you to be surprised." I stand behind her, covering a palm over her eyes.

"Ayden! Is this really necessary? I'm gonna trip and fall on my ass."

"I'd never let that happen," I whisper above her ear. "Trust me?"

She blows out a breath, shuddering against me. "Okay."

My other hand squeezes her hip and directs her to keep walking straight ahead. The thin material of her shirt has my fingers itching to touch her bare skin.

"Just keep goin'. Almost there." I keep my chest pressed to her back so we walk in sync.

"This better be an amazin' view," she chastises, and I chuckle.

"Trust me, it's already good from here."

She playfully elbows my gut, and I grunt.

"Ready?" I finally ask when we stand in the perfect spot.

When she nods, I drop my hand but don't step away. Glancing at her face, I watch as her eyes widen and her lips part.

"Wow...you can see so much of the ranch up here."

"Look behind us," I say, and we shift. "The retreat cabins are over there."

"Damn. I wish I hadn't seen this. Now I'll never wanna leave."

"I was lucky to find this place when I did," I admit, thinking back to when I was desperate to find a job.

"Maybe we can bring Serena here before she goes back to school in the fall." Laney turns and asks.

"I'd love that. Could you take off work?"

"If I have coverage, yeah."

Taking her hand, I lead her to the decorated rocks Mallory and Noah painted a year ago, and we sit.

"Can you tell me about Howie's life? Did he stay workin' at his dad's garage?" I ask when we settle in next to each other.

"Yeah, he practically took over by the time he passed. Jimmy was gettin' too old and tired of the long hours in the heat. Serena and I stopped in a lot to bring them lunch. She adores Jim."

"So everyone in town knew she was mine and figured I'd just abandoned you?" The thought has a knife slicing through my heart.

"Ayden..." She stammers, but my phone interrupts.

"Shit, sorry. It's Tripp."

She flashes a small smile while I answer it.

"Yeah?"

"Disco's on the loose. It's all hands on deck. Can ya help?"

"Fuck. How'd that happen?" I shake my head.

"Little shit knows how to wiggle the lock with his nose, and I was in the tack room. He was long gone before I noticed."

I snort. "Oops, shoulda warned ya about him."

"Yeah, thanks. Can you come or what?"

"I'm up on Sunset Trail, but I'll look for him while I drive back."

"Sounds good. Text if you see him."

"Got it."

I end the call and sigh. "Sorry, duty calls."

"It's okay. What happened?" she asks while we walk to the four-wheeler.

"Disco's a new boarder and too smart for his own good. He got out and is probably grazin' in a pasture somewhere."

"What're you gonna do if you find him?"

"Depends on where he is, but I'll let Tripp know, and he can figure it out. Unfortunately, this isn't the first time a horse's gotten out, and we've had to chase it down."

Once we're riding on the trail again, Laney holds on to me even tighter as I take another route, one closer to the pastures. He couldn't have gone far.

"Ah, there he is." I point to our right. He's rolling around in a mud bath.

"Oh my God." She laughs. "I didn't know horses did that."

"It cools them down. But that gate should've been closed since it flooded back here. Twenty bucks one of the twins left it open."

"Double it, and I'll put my bet on Wilder," she mocks, and I crack up at how quickly she's caught on.

"No way, I'll lose."

I drive closer to the fence and whistle, hoping to get his attention. Taking out my phone, I text Tripp the location, and he sends back an ETA of five minutes.

"Disco," I call out, turning off the engine. Laney and I remove our helmets and set them on the seat. My attempts to get his attention fail, but at least he's not running.

"I bet you have a different adventure each day," she says, staring at Disco as he continues acting like a pig in mud.

"Oh yeah. It's never the same 'round here. Always some shit goin' on. Makes it fun, though sometimes it's stressful, too."

"I bet."

"I never asked. Did you stay workin' at your mom's boutique?"

"Yeah, I basically took over and spent years adding more inventory so we'd attract more tourists. Finally, it worked, and we were able to hire some part-time workers."

"That's amazin', Lane."

Her mom opened a shop filled with specialty clothes and accessories. It was her high school weekend job, and last I knew, they were struggling to keep it open.

Smiling wide, she nods. "I have pictures of me baby-wearing Serena while I'd do inventory after hours. She'd never sleep unless she was on my chest, so I had to get creative."

Now I'm the one smiling. "I have no doubt you're an incredible mom."

"I love being her mom. It came naturally, more than I thought it would, but it was almost like we grew up together. Only being eighteen with a newborn, my friends couldn't relate, so eventually, they stopped invitin' me out. When she was three, she was a little gabber mouth and so much fun to play with. I much preferred to hang out with her than go out drinkin'."

I can't stop beaming at the imagery of Laney and Serena at those ages.

"And now you're twenty-eight, and she's already halfway to being an adult."

Her eyes widen in panic, and she nudges me. "Hush your mouth. Don't say that."

Chuckling, I wrap an arm around her shoulders and pull her into my chest. "I like that y'all are close. Hopefully, someday, I can have that with her, too."

Tripp comes sprinting on Mallory's horse and frowns. "Jesus Christ. He's gonna need a bath."

I smirk. "Hope you brought your rain boots."

"Fuck you. This is supposed to be your shift, not mine."

"He got loose on your watch," I remind him.

"Whatever." He finally darts his gaze to Laney. "You must be Ayden's secret lady friend Wilder won't shut up about. I'm Tripp."

"Nice to meet you," Laney replies.

"You got this handled now?" I ask.

"Yeah, yeah." He digs his heel and leads Miss Swift toward

Disco. Tripp manages to wrap a rope around his neck and bring him closer as he rides out of the pasture.

"He can bring him back on his own?" Laney asks.

"As long as Disco doesn't fight it, he'll be fine. I should lock that gate, though."

We hop back on the four-wheeler and drive to the open fence. Once it's secure, I ask Laney if she's tired.

"Yeah, I think I should probably go back to my hotel room. It's been a long day."

She flew in this morning and spent the afternoon with me, so I don't blame her, but I selfishly want to spend more time with her.

"I'll drop you off at your car. You'll come back tomorrow?"

"Sure, but I have to leave before lunch to make my flight."

I hate that she can't stay longer, but I understand she has our daughter and a job to get back to.

And Howie's funeral.

I bring us to my truck and then drive her back. We make small talk, and when we're in the parking lot, neither of us moves to get out.

"Thank you for comin' to find me. I wasn't sure I'd ever see you again," I admit.

She doesn't meet my eyes. "Truthfully, I wasn't sure I would either. I was scared you wouldn't want to."

Leaning over, I tilt up her chin until our gazes collide. "I'm sorry I ever made you believe that, but now that you're back in my life, I'm not going anywhere. We'll figure something out so I can come down to visit, and when it's feasible, I'll fly you two up here. Okay?"

She bites down on her bottom lip, nodding.

"Meet me for breakfast? I'll be here at nine."

My break isn't until eleven thirty, but I'll get one of the guys to cover for me.

"That works."

I brush my mouth against her cheek, silently wishing she'd turn an inch so I could taste her lips, but when she doesn't move, I lean back. "Night, Laney. Drive safe."

"G'night, Ayden."

She jumps out and walks to her rental car. The scent of her coconut shampoo lingers in the air, and I inhale deeply at the familiarity. Once she's inside and buckled, she gives me a little wave, and I almost instinctively honk my horn three times but then stop myself. I take that as my cue to drive off before I do something stupid.

Chapter Four

Laney

The moment his rearview lights are out of view, I exhale and lean back against my headrest.

Being that close to Ayden brings back too many memories of when we couldn't keep our hands off each other. He used any excuse to touch me, and I'd let him.

A part of me wanted him to kiss me, but the other part knew I couldn't handle it.

I'm not staying, and he can't leave his safe place.

We'd be two ships in the night passing each other, but neither willing to stick around.

He'll visit his daughter but never plant roots in Texas again, not as long as his father's alive.

My mom and job keep me there. It's where Serena grew up and all she knows, plus all her friends.

And now, it's where Howie's buried.

Uprooting our lives would be a risk.

But why do I want to risk it all for a second chance at a life we were supposed to have together?

Once I return to my hotel room, I shower and change into

clean, comfy clothes. Then I FaceTime Serena and my mom to tell them good night.

"Did you find him, Mommy?" Serena asks.

"Yeah, sweetie. I did."

Her face lights up, filled with hope and excitement. "Did you tell him about me?"

My mom's expression behind her stays impassive. She's worried we'll get hurt again.

"Sure did. Showed him lots of photos, too."

"Is he gonna visit?"

"Yes, in a few weeks."

"Not for the funeral?" my mom asks.

I shake my head. "He has to work," I tell her, but she can read between the lines.

"I'm so excited!" Serena squeals.

When I explained that I'd be leaving for a couple of days, she wanted to know why. She knew Ayden's name and overheard me talking about him to my mom, so when she asked if I was going to find her daddy, I couldn't lie. She's old enough to understand some of it, but I kept the details of her paternal grandparents out of the story.

Although Bryant Carson isn't the mayor anymore, he's still a powerful figure in Beaumont. Everyone knows the Carsons and that Serena is Ayden's, but no one dared to ask why he left or why I married Howie. Rumor mills spread like wildfire, but we pretended they didn't exist. It was no one's business, but people had their theories.

"You be good for Nana, okay? I'll be home tomorrow for supper."

"Okay, Mommy. Love you!"

"I love you, too."

We blow kisses until my mom ends the call. If it were up to Serena, we'd say good night for hours.

After my divorce, I was ready for a fresh start, and even though dating afterward didn't work out, I never had the urge to get close to another man. However, it took one touch from Ayden for goose bumps to cover my skin and heat to build between my legs.

A part of me was relieved I wasn't broken.

The other part was too damn close to begging him to touch me again.

Just as I'm tossing and turning, struggling to fall asleep, my room phone rings.

I nearly scream at the unexpected loudness.

"Hello?" I sit on the edge of the bed, waiting.

"Laney, it's me."

I chuckle. "You scared me."

"Sorry. I forgot to get your number and wanted to make sure you made it there safely."

"I did, but wait...how'd you know where I was stayin'?"

He blows out an amused laugh. "I'm about to admit something very embarrassing."

Chuckling low, I snuggle under the covers with the phone pressed to my ear.

"I'm listenin'."

"I may have called five other hotels before someone directed me to your room."

My brows rise. "Isn't that a violation of guests' privacy?"

"Well...I might've used my Southern charm to sway the receptionist."

I snort. "Still insufferable, I see."

"Am not! Persistent," he counters.

"Mm-Hmm. What'd you say?"

"Explained to them someone at the retreat had left their passport. I only knew you were stayin' at one of the hotels in town but wasn't sure which one and that it was urgent I found you before you got to the airport."

I wrinkle my nose at his lame story. "And she bought that?"

"Well, *sweetheart*..." He emphasizes his drawl. "I can be very persuasive."

Rolling my eyes, I laugh because I know firsthand how convincing Ayden Carson can be.

"I guess we better exchange numbers so you don't have to charm any more receptionists."

"Is that jealousy I hear?" His mocking tone has me biting back a smile.

"No, it's *concern*. You could've gotten that woman fired for seducin' information out of her."

He bellows out a laugh. "Fuck, I've missed you. Even when I devoted every minute of my life to you, that little hint of jealousy would still come out."

"I hate you." I pout, leaning against the headboard.

"You don't," he murmurs.

He's right. I could never hate him, even when there were times I wanted to.

I force out a yawn. "You ready for my number? I'm fallin' asleep."

"Yes, please."

I ramble off the digits, and moments later, my cell vibrates with his message.

"Now you have mine."

"Perfect. I'll see you in the mornin' then," I say.

"Sweet dreams, Laney."

"G'night."

I hang up the phone and blow out a breath to slow my racing heart.

Years later, he still flusters me.

In the bathroom, I look at my flushed face and shake my head. I'm being a silly teenage girl all over again.

I brush my teeth, wash my face, and grab my phone to set my alarm.

It's then I read his message.

AYDEN

You're still so goddamn beautiful.

My fingers itch to type out a response, but I know we'll stay up texting, and it'll lead to something we can't have. My heart is already on edge with suppressed feelings I've spent years pushing away, but after one day with Ayden, they're fighting their way back in.

After a restless night, I finally slide out of bed at eight and get ready to meet Ayden. Then I pack up my bags and check out. My flight is at two, which means I need to leave at eleven thirty to get to the airport on time. As much as I wish I could spend another day with him and spill the secrets I need to share, I miss Serena like crazy. I know she'll ask for all the details, and we'll spend the next few weeks anticipating Ayden's arrival back in Texas.

She's going to fall in love with him. Inevitably, he will with her as well. It's not only my heart on the line. Now it's our daughter's, too.

Chapter Five

Ayden

The moment I walk into The Lodge, I spot Laney sitting at a table being harassed by Wilder.

Of-fucking-course.

That little shit is going to eat my fist for breakfast if he gets another inch closer.

"Mornin'," I greet before I reach her, then lean down and brush my lips against her cheek. "He botherin' you?" I whisper in her ear.

"I was just sayin' hello," Wilder argues.

Crossing my arms over my chest, I narrow my eyes at him. "And now ya did, so get on outta here."

Laney grabs my arm. "He was just tellin' me about the ranch and all the work he does 'round here."

"Wilder?" I snort, glaring at him as he shoots me a mischievous grin. "He's about as helpful as a pogo stick in quicksand."

"Now you know that ain't true. You're just torn up that I got to her before you did." He mimics my stance, knowing I won't cause a scene in front of the guests eating.

"And now you're leavin'. Goodbye."

"It was nice meetin' ya, Miss Laney. Hope to see ya again real soon." Wilder tips his ball cap and flashes her a flirty smirk before meeting my glare. "Just remember, God don't like ugly, Ayden."

Then he flips me the bird before finally getting lost.

"You two have a beef or what?" Laney asks, standing from her chair.

I grunt, remembering the *drama* from a few months ago. "You could say that. How'd you sleep?"

"Not great, but I never do in hotel beds." She shrugs it off.

"Sorry to hear that. I have a spare room you could've slept in, but I didn't wanna interrupt your plans."

"That's alright. I'll be home by supper and should be passed out by nine."

"Let's get you some food before your flight. Hope you're hungry. They feed ya like it's your last meal here." I take her hand and lead her toward the buffet.

"I love the theme of this place. Everything looks so genuine and rustic."

"Garrett and Dena love their horses." I snicker. "Reminded me of home the first time I walked in. Probably why I liked it so much."

"I can see that. Remember the time Brandi's horse followed her all the way to school, and Mr. Williams had to give her a pass to walk it back to her ranch?"

I bellow out a laugh. "Shit, yeah, I do. Took her an hour to return."

"At that point, I would've just stayed home."

We each pile food on our plates filled with biscuits and gravy, grits, eggs, and sausage. Then I grab two mugs of hot coffee and bring them back to our table.

"Thank you," she says, adding two little creamers.

"Still don't drink it black, huh?" I taunt.

"No way." She smirks, glancing at my plate.

"What? I'm a big boy now." I pat my stomach.

Laney chuckles, and the sound goes right into my chest. "Just not used to seein' you eat so much. Not used to thinkin' of you as a cowboy."

"Howie and I played plenty of cowboy games."

"You mean the two of you wrestling and tryin' to put each other in headlocks?"

I laugh as I shove a forkful of food in my mouth. She's not wrong.

"I remember there being props," I defend. "We just had more fun tryin' to kill each other."

Laney's gaze lowers to her plate, and I worry I hit a sore spot. I'm not sure how close they were after I left, but his death obviously affected her.

"Lane," I murmur, reaching over and squeezing her thigh.

When she looks up, tears form in her eyes. I hate the pain behind them and wish I could take it away.

"I'm okay. Just rememberin' all the fun the three of us had as kids. Every memory through graduation had you and Howie in it."

I nod, feeling the guilt slice up my spine at how I never kept in touch once I left. Though I was determined to have that clean slate, I should've thought more about what it'd do to the ones who loved me.

"He thought you'd come back," she says as if she's read my thoughts. "The day after you left, he was convinced you'd turn around. After a week, he said you probably got lost and would make your way back. After three months, he said there was no way you'd last another three. After a year, he stopped makin' guesses. A part of him—and me—thought you'd walk through the door again."

The pain laced in her voice eats me inside.

"I'd thought about it a million times, Laney. I really did. I almost called both of you a hundred times. I was so scared my dad would find me. I knew it was unlikely, but I couldn't stand the thought of him somehow tracin' your phones to get to me."

He did it to mine, so there was no reason not to think he'd do it to them too.

After what I witnessed him do in high school, I wouldn't put anything past him to make sure we stayed quiet.

"We can't rewrite the past, Ayden. I understand why you thought you had to do it." She squeezes my hand that's still resting on her leg. "I FaceTimed with Serena and my mom last night. Told them I found ya."

I swallow hard, going back to my food. "Yeah? What'd they say?"

"Serena was so excited she nearly jumped through the screen. She can't wait to meet you. It makes my heart so happy to know she will soon."

"I still can't wrap my head around us havin' a kid, Lane. But God, I'm glad I get to make up for it in some small way."

"She'll steal your heart the moment you meet. I can promise ya that." She smirks, and I have no doubt. The same way Laney always has.

As we continue eating, we talk about the people I once knew back home and the new ones I met when I moved here.

"So we only have a couple hours until you have to go. Can I give you a tour of the retreat part of the ranch? Then maybe I can show you the main house if there's time. I'm sure Dena would love to meet you."

I'm surprised she hasn't bombarded me already.

"I'd love that! It looked beautiful on the website," she admits. "Serena was beggin' me to take her so she could sleep in one of the cabins."

I chuckle, taking our empty dishes and putting them in the bin. "I'm sure I can arrange that sometime. They have tons of activities for kids here."

Like a couple who's done it a million times, our hands gravitate toward one another, and our fingers interlock as we walk to my truck.

"Who makes the food here?" she asks as I drive us down one of the gravel roads.

"Garrett's aunts. They've been cooks here since they opened the retreat nearly twenty years ago. Dena has some family who does various jobs around the ranch, too. Some of the cousins work at the saloon, some do housekeeping, and then some are in charge of the family activities at the retreat. It's a whole family affair."

"Wow, that's cool. What are the parents in charge of?"

"Dena's at home mostly. She cooks for the ranch hands and staff so they don't have to worry about comin' up to The Lodge and eatin' during guest hours. Her mom lives there too, so between the two of them in the kitchen, their house smells like a Southern café and bakery all hours of the day."

"Is that where you normally go eat?"

"Not every day, but three or four times a week. Otherwise, I make a sandwich at home. Just depends on how busy I am. Sometimes I wait it out until supper."

"What does her husband do?"

"Garrett manages most of the paperwork and financials. They have a business manager, but everything goes through him. Noah wanted to expand the training quarters and pleaded with him for five months, plus gave a presentation on how it'd benefit the ranch."

"Goodness."

"Don't worry, Noah gave it her all and even outdid her projected earnings. Now he lets her do whatever she wants since she's earned it. Her four brothers, however, not so much."

She chuckles. "They don't seem so bad. Typical rowdy cowboys with hearts of gold."

"Don't tell me you're buying that fake charm shit they've been layin' on ya?"

"Don't tell me you're jealous?"

I give her a pointed look. "You're dodgin' my question."

"You're dodgin' mine," she retorts, and I scoff. "I think you never grew up with brothers and have spent the past decade experiencing what it was like. Sounds like typical sibling rivalry to me."

Shrugging, I keep my eyes on the road as we get closer to the retreat's entrance. "Maybe."

It's not that I don't consider them my family, but I haven't been able to let them in as close as I want, given my own parents. The two people who were supposed to protect and love me unconditionally were the ones I feared the most. The ones who made me run in the first place and leave the love of my life and a child I never knew about.

"Okay, here we are..." I nod toward her window and drive slower. "On the right is the pool and lounge area, and next to it is the huge bonfire. They light it every Friday night and have a s'mores party for everyone."

"That sounds delicious. I haven't had one of those in years."

"Probably since we made them in high school, huh?"

"Yep. Serena would love them, though."

"The barn and pasture for the trail horses are down that

way." I point. "The trail rides are behind the cabins up the hill to the left. Wilder and Waylon do them twice a day."

"I bet they're a hoot to have as guides," she says with a knowing grin. "In a non-charming way."

"Mm-Hmm." I roll my eyes.

"They were in one of those bridal party videos too. I recognized their faces but didn't wanna say anything in front of them. They were rippin' off their shirts and givin' lap dances like a cowboy straight outta *Magic Mike*."

I groan at the imagery. "Of course they were."

"I thought you joined a ranch strip club." She fails at holding back a laugh when I shoot her a murderous glare. "There's five cabins, right?"

"Yeah. The two larger ones sleep up to twelve people and the other three sleep up to six."

"That's a good number."

"Yeah, not too many at once, and even at the bare minimum, enough to keep the staff busy. Wanna stop and look around or go to the main house?"

"I'd love to meet the Hollises if you don't mind going there?"

"Not at all. When you come back with Serena, we'll go ridin' as a family." I glance over and notice a red tint over her cheeks.

"I'd love that," she says.

Me too.

Once I park in front of the two-story sage-colored house, we get out and meet in front of my truck.

"This is the perfect country house." Laney admires the immaculate landscaping and wraparound porch filled with rocking chairs and hanging plants. "I wonder if they sit out here a lot."

"Gramma Grace and Dena do after supper. They like to read and enjoy the peace and quiet after the kitchen's cleaned up and everyone's left to do their evening chores," I tell her. "That's been their mother-daughter tradition ever since she moved in three years ago after her father passed away."

"Oh, how sad. How many live here?"

I start counting on my fingers. "Gramma Grace, Garrett and Dena, Landen, and Tripp. Also Mallory, who took over Noah's bedroom when she moved in last year. You haven't met her yet, but she's their little cousin."

"The twins live in the ranch hand cabins by you. Where's Noah stayin'?"

"She has a cottage about half a mile away. Noah likes having her privacy and being away from her brothers."

She laughs. "Understandable."

Grabbing her hand, I lead her up the porch stairs and open the door. "Knock, knock. Comin' in," I call out.

"Is that my favorite Texas cowboy?" Dena asks.

Chuckling, I shake my head. "Always tryin' to butter me up, ain't ya?"

"Well, I gotta." She turns around from the sink and smiles at me, then notices Laney and her eyes widen. "I was wonderin' when you were gonna let me meet your guest."

"Laney, this is Dena Hollis. Dena, this is Laney Bennett."

"The high school girlfriend, right?" Dena wipes her hands off on a towel and unties her apron.

Laney snickers. "That's my reputation 'round here now, ain't it?"

"Accordin' to my sources, yes."

I snort. "You mean Wilder."

"Please sit. I'll serve sweet tea. Want anything to eat?"

"We ate already, but thank you," I tell her.

For the next hour, Dena talks our ears off while asking Laney twenty questions. She nearly spits out her sweet tea when she learns about Serena and demands Laney and her move here. I want to ask her to do the same thing, but I have no right to do that.

When it gets close to Laney's time to leave, we thank Dena again, and Laney promises she'll see her again soon.

"Oh, Ayden. I'm fixin' to go to the store this afternoon. It's your turn to pick this Sunday's menu."

"You spoil me. I'll text you in an hour," I tell her so I don't lose any more alone time with Laney.

She shoots me a wink, and I lead Laney out to my truck.

"She's really sweet, Ayden," she says once we head back to The Lodge.

"Like the mother I never had."

Laney reaches out and squeezes my thigh. "Good. You deserve that."

"When you're here next, I'll make sure you meet Garrett. You'll like him. Looks like one of those beefed-up cowboys from the show *Yellowstone*. Guests are always tellin' him how much he looks like that one guy..."

"Rip Wheeler!" she squeals.

I crack up laughing. "Of course you're a fan."

"Mama and I binged it. She kept tellin' me we needed some cowboys in our lives."

"Got plenty of those here." I shoot her a wink.

Her lips arch. "I've noticed."

"Never seen an episode in my life, yet I know way too much about that damn show thanks to Noah and her best friend, Magnolia, talkin' about it nonstop."

Laney smirks. "Trust me, it's worth the hype."

"I don't need to watch a show about ranch life when I live it each day."

She smirks, shaking her head. "Still stubborn as I remember, too."

Grabbing her hand from my thigh, I embrace it in mine and then brush my lips across her knuckles. "And you're just as beautiful as I remember."

Chapter Six
Laney

Ayden Carson swept me off my feet in ninth grade when he performed a whole promposal and kissed me in front of the cheerleading squad. Fourteen years later, a simple kiss on my hand has me feeling the same way.

"I'm really happy you found me and came here, Laney," he tells me when he parks beside my rental car. I've been dreading this moment since I woke up this morning.

"So am I," I admit. It's on the tip of my tongue to tell him one of the secrets he'll inevitably learn once he comes to Beaumont, but I'm too scared it'll make him change his mind about visiting.

We didn't talk nearly enough about what he's missed the past ten years, and once we do, it'll change everything.

"I'll get with Garrett to get time off within the next few weeks. Do you want me to book a hotel?"

"Oh, um...no. Serena would love for you to stay with us."

And so would I.

He nods. "Okay. Will you text me when you get home so I know you made it safely?"

I smile. "Of course."

When he reaches for his door handle and jumps out, I do the same. As I wait for him to come around, butterflies in my stomach have me ready to throw up. I hated saying goodbye to him ten years ago, and I hate it just as much today.

Ayden approaches and swarms me in a hug. His thick arms envelop my body and press me to his chest as if I were a puzzle piece made to fit perfectly into his. I wrap mine around his waist, grasping tightly to his T-shirt, and then inhale his cologne. My breath catches when he leans down and presses his lips to my forehead, placing a soft, subtle kiss there. For a moment, I think about lifting my head so my mouth collides with his, but then he steps away too quickly, and my moment to decide dissipates.

"Have a safe flight, Laney." He opens my door for me and waits until I'm buckled in before closing it. Then he flashes a boyish smile and gives me a gentle wave before walking back to his truck.

The heaviness in my chest doesn't fade until long after I'm on my flight. The anticipation of seeing Serena floods my veins. The only time we've spent a night apart is when she's had sleepovers, but she was only five minutes away. Being states apart spiked my anxiety even though I knew she was in good hands.

As soon as the plane lands in Houston, I turn on my phone and check my messages.

AYDEN

> I was being a gentleman this time, but when I see you next, I might not have the willpower to keep my lips off yours. I hope you have a good flight.

Come With Me

My heart lodges in my throat as I reread his message for the fifth time. How can he just shoot out these one-liners and think they won't affect me? How am I even supposed to respond?

How do I even begin to comprehend that my feelings for him never faded? Though we're different people now with very different lives, I haven't forgotten what his touches feel like.

> **LANEY**
> I just landed. Flight went great.

> **AYDEN**
> Glad to hear it. Drive safe back home :)

> **LANEY**
> How is it you're even more charming now than you were back in high school?

> **AYDEN**
> Aw, you think I'm charming, do ya?

I roll my eyes.

> **LANEY**
> You know you are.

If we were being honest, that's what got me pregnant in the first place. We couldn't keep our hands off each other.

> **AYDEN**
> I can promise that it's only ever been for you.
> No one else.

The heart that was in my throat moments ago sinks to the pit of my stomach. I'm battling whether to guard my heart or allow myself to open it back up to the man who tore it apart before. *Am I strong enough to give Ayden another chance?*

LANEY

I want to trust you, Ayden. I really do. But you broke my heart, and I'm scared you'll do it again.

AYDEN

I know, sweetheart. I have a lot of making up to do, and I promise I won't stop until I do.

I send him a blushing-face emoji, then send my mom a message to let her know I'll be in baggage claim soon.

As soon as I grab my carry-on and walk off the plane, I'm eager to find them.

"Mom!" I hear Serena shout. She rushes toward me with her arms open and slams into me.

"Hey, baby!" I squeeze her tight. "You grew an inch overnight!"

"I did not!" She pulls back and looks up at me. "I missed you."

"I missed you too." I kiss the top of her head.

"You two are inseparable." My mom chuckles.

It's true. Even with Howie around, Serena and I always took on the world together.

Once I grab my suitcase, Serena takes my hand and leads me out to the car.

"Tell me *everythin'*," she says dramatically once we buckle in. "What's it like up in *Ten-naw-see*?" she purposely drags out the word, making me laugh.

"Pretty similar to Texas," I admit. "I met a lot of the family there."

"Don't they have the best accents?" my mom asks with a grin.

I chuckle and nod.

"They don't talk like us?" Serena asks.

"They do, but they have more of a twang in theirs, and it's more distinctive."

"Do I get to go up there?"

"Yeah, baby. Eventually. Ayden's gonna come here first in a few weeks."

"Oh my gosh. Can we go to the beach? And a rodeo? And the zoo? Will he be here for the Fourth of July?" Her whole face lights up as she bounces in her seat.

"Sweetheart, slow down. Once he finalizes the dates he can come, we'll make plans for all that, okay?"

I love that she wants to experience so many fun, family-filled days, but I worry her heart will shatter as soon as he leaves. It's not hard to fall in love with Ayden, and I have no doubt she'll love him the moment she meets him.

"Is he excited to meet me?" Serena asks.

"*So* excited, baby."

Mom catches me up on store stuff between Serena coming up with more things for us to do. A giddy smile stays plastered on her face for the rest of the ride home. I can't stop replaying every interaction we had over the past twenty-four hours.

I only hope we get many more.

Chapter Seven

Ayden

For the past three weeks, I've felt like a new man.

A new reason to get up in the morning.

A new reason to smile.

And it's due to two ladies who have my heart in a chokehold.

I didn't want to wait to officially meet Serena in person, so I asked Laney if we could FaceTime and to help ease the nerves for when we are face-to-face. I wanted to get to know her a little before invading their home for a week. Then, in the evenings, I'd text Laney and thank her over and over for giving me this chance to be in their lives.

Talking Garrett into letting me have time off was easy, considering I'd never taken a vacation in the decade I've worked at the ranch, but getting people to cover my job was another story. This is our busy season, and with it being hot as fuck already, no one wants to put in the extra hours.

It's safe to say I owe a few ranch hands a kidney and liver if they ever need one.

Come With Me

Wilder demanded Laney's phone number in exchange for cleaning stalls, and a punch to his gut was my answer.

For the next seven days, my only concern is meeting my daughter and hopefully repairing some of the damage my disappearance has done. Although the three of us have spoken nearly every night, I'm still nervous as hell being in Texas. I've no idea what people will think about me being back or why they think I left in the first place. My dad will no doubt hear about my return and find a way to invade, or best-case scenario, he'll have disappeared too.

My nerves spiked the entire two-and-a-half-hour flight, and when we finally land, I inhale a deep breath and prepare for my entire life to change.

AYDEN

Walking off the plane now. Where should I meet you?

LANEY

Don't worry, you'll see us ;-)

Furrowing my brow, I walk toward baggage claim and wonder what she means. There's no need to be concerned, though, because as soon as I go down the escalators, I see two beautiful ladies waiting for me.

Laney's gaze meets mine as she smiles wide, and next to her stands Serena with half a dozen balloons with a variety of *Happy Birthday Dad* and *Happy Father's Day* written on them. Laney holds up a large piece of white plasterboard that reads: *Picking up the hottest cowboy in Texas.* And it's decorated with pictures of Laney and Serena.

"I can't believe y'all did this." I shake my head with the biggest smile on my face as I walk toward them.

Laney shrugs modestly. "Serena demanded a welcomin' party."

Kneeling in front of Serena, I take her free hand. "Thank you. It's so nice to meet ya in person finally."

"May I hug you?"

"Are you kiddin'? Of course."

My arms open as she falls into them. The balloons smack us in the face, and she giggles as I laugh.

"Since we missed birthdays and Father's Day, Mom said we could get them for you," she says, pulling back.

"I love them. Thank you." I kiss the top of her hand. "I'll treasure them forever."

Standing, I pull Laney into a hug next and sigh at how good it feels to have her back in my arms. "Thank you." Then I cup her cheek and mold my mouth to hers.

I warned her I wouldn't be so polite next time, and although I couldn't wait to kiss her, I don't get too carried away since Serena is next to us and we're in a public place. But the thought is definitely there.

Sliding my tongue between her lips, I stroke hers with mine briefly before pulling away.

She blinks up at me, stunned into silence, her chest rapidly moving up and down.

"You taste like strawberry," I murmur with a grin and loving the way her face flushes.

"Um...so how's it feel being back in Texas?" she asks after a beat of silence and noticing Serena staring at us.

"Best first impression I've ever had." I shoot her a wink. "In terms of everythin' else, I'll let you know in a few."

I'm still nervous as hell.

Going from nine hundred miles away to being back in my hometown gives me mixed feelings. I half expect my dad to pop out of somewhere and tell me what a piece of shit I am for not being here for my kid.

As if he's the poster child for being a father.

We walk to the carousel and grab my bag. Once we're at the car, I fight to get the balloons in the back seat, and Serena loses her mind laughing as each one hits me in the face. Eventually, she takes pity on me and helps.

As we drive to their house, Serena talks about anything and everything. I can't stop smiling as I stare at her face. She looks so much like Laney, although she tells me she thinks Serena has my nose. Either way, she's beautiful inside and out.

"So tomorrow, we'll go to the zoo and have a picnic with the hippos. Then—"

"*With* the hippos?" I raise a brow.

"They're my favorite animal!" she exclaims.

"Oh, then we must eat with them!" I flash her a wink.

She goes on and on until we finally arrive. I love how excited she is because it reassures me I didn't make a mistake in coming here. Laney helps with my bags and balloons before we go inside.

Serena's eager to give me a house tour. It's much nicer than I was expecting since I know Laney's been on a single income since her divorce. She hasn't brought up her marriage or what happened, and I haven't asked her about it, but I hope she will when she's ready.

"C'mon, I wanna show you my room!" Serena grabs my hand and pulls me down a hallway.

"Serena Mae, slow down!" Laney shouts from the living room, and Serena giggles in return.

She whips open the door, and I smile at the beautiful wall artwork of ladybugs and butterflies. She has posters lined up next to her bunk bed and a dresser on the other side with a small TV.

"This is adorable," I tell her, noticing the LED lights on the ceiling.

"Check this out!" She turns on a black device. It splashes lights and stars across the ceiling. "It's my galaxy machine."

"Whoa, this is the coolest room I've ever seen! Do I get to sleep in here?"

"Yeah, like a slumber party!" she squeals.

"Actually, you can have my bed," Laney says, approaching the doorway.

Serena frowns, and so do I. The last thing I wanted to do was put her out.

"He's too big for that little bed, sweetie. I'll sleep in here with you."

"Are you sure?" I look at her. "I don't mind."

She puts a hand on my shoulder. "Trust me, you'll thank me tomorrow when you don't wake up with a kinked neck."

I resist the urge to tell her we can share *her* bed, but I'm definitely thinking it.

"Let me show you the rest of the house," Laney insists.

She leads me to the guest bathroom, shows off her office, and then finally, the master suite. I set my suitcase and carry-on down before looking around.

"This is so nice, Laney. Very you." I smirk. Pictures of Serena cover the walls. Some with her and some with her mother. Small house plants are on the windowsill, and artificial ivy vines twist around the curtain rod.

"Thanks. I really wanted it to be a safe, relaxin' place at the end of a busy workday. After Serena's in bed, I take a long, hot bath and unwind for a bit. It's my favorite place in the house."

She shows me her bathroom with a deep tub and standing shower.

"Good. You deserve that." It's on the tip of my tongue to ask if her ex lived here too. "When did you move here?"

She scratches at her throat. "Um, I guess it's been about eight years."

So the ex did live here.

"Well, you've made it into a very nice home for Serena."

With a small smile, she nods, then leads me toward the kitchen.

"Serena and I make dinner together every night I'm not workin'. She's really excited to cook with you."

"I'm not much of a cook," I tell her.

"Serena loves it. When she's at my mom's, they make a feast. She's gettin' pretty good for her age."

I grin at that. "I hope she doesn't mind teachin' me then."

That evening, Laney and I order in Chinese food after Serena passes out for the night. After Serena taught me how to make French toast for dinner, we played board games, and then they showed me several family albums. It was the most normal family evening I've ever had, and I loved every minute of it.

"So can I ask you about something?" I ask as we eat. Though we ate with Serena earlier, we were both still hungry.

"Yeah, sure."

"What happened with your marriage?" I blurt out.

She swallows hard at my unexpected question. "Um...well. We were more like roommates. But truthfully, I wanted—"

"Mom!" Serena screams, and we both jump.

"Comin'!"

I follow Laney as she rushes toward Serena's room.

"What is it, baby?" Laney asks while I wait by the doorframe.

"I had a nightmare."

"Oh, sweetie. You're okay. It was just a dream." Laney sits on the edge of the bed, running her fingers through Serena's hair. "Do you want me to stay until you fall asleep?"

Serena nods. "Can Dad too?"

My heart pounds at hearing her call me *dad*. On the phone, I introduced myself as Ayden, and it's what she's called me until now. Honestly, I wasn't expecting it and am overjoyed at how quickly she's adjusted to me being in their lives.

"Sure, kiddo." I walk in and kneel next to the bed.

"She likes her head massaged," Laney tells me.

I smile wide. "I can do that."

Chapter Eight
Laney

When Ayden asked about my marriage, I fully intended to tell him the truth. If Serena hadn't interrupted, I would've, but now I don't know how to bring up the subject without ruining our time together. It's a secret that has eaten at me since we reunited. I plan to tell him before he leaves, but I'm not sure how. I'm not worried about him not understanding. I'm more concerned with how he'll retaliate and the consequences of his actions.

Today's a day Serena's been looking forward to, so I don't want anything to wreck it. She loves the zoo, and we spent an hour this morning packing our lunches.

"Are you excited, Dad?" Serena asks as she bounces in the back seat. She's been calling him that all morning, and it warms my heart. She's known about Ayden for so long. It's surreal she finally gets to have him here.

"So excited," he exclaims. "I can't wait to pet a hippo."

"What?" she screeches, giggling. "You can't pet them!"

"I can't? Why not?"

She giggles again, shaking her head as if he doesn't know better.

"They'll eat you!"

Their banter is the cutest thing I've ever witnessed.

Howie had a great relationship with Serena. He was the male role model in her life that she needed at the time, and I know he'd be so happy and proud that Ayden's back in our lives.

I just wish he were alive now to see it.

Five hours and an exhausted child later, we walk into the house. Serena fell asleep on the drive home, and Ayden offered to carry her in so we didn't have to wake her. He's slipped so easily into this dad role, it's going to be even harder when he has to leave.

As I unpack our leftovers, I talk to my mom on the phone, who wanted an update about our family day out. I gave her the condensed version of everything we did and how much fun we had. When I hear Ayden coming down the hallway, I tell her goodbye and hang up.

"Alright, she's tucked in and snorin' away." Ayden walks into the kitchen in a change of comfy clothes.

He looks worn out, too, though I don't blame him. Serena's energy can take a while to get used to. She had us walking all over the place, to the gift shop and then back around for a second lap. We each held Serena's hands as she talked nonstop about hippos, monkeys, and snakes. She loves to read, so bringing her to the boutique with me was always easy. She'd stay in my office and get lost in animal books.

"She had the best day with you today," I tell him, wiping down the counter.

He leans against the doorframe with a smile on his too-perfect face. "So did I, and now I can't wait to show her 'round the ranch."

"She's gonna love it so much," I agree.

"Mallory's a couple years older, and she'll enjoy showin' her the ropes."

"The niece, right?"

"Yep. She lost both of her parents last year, and being around horses has been therapeutic for her. Noah tells me she's still grieving pretty hard, but she puts on a strong front."

"Wow. How sad." I'd be devastated to lose my mom. I can't even imagine losing both parents at once.

He pushes off the doorframe and stalks toward me. "So what do you do for yourself?"

"What do you mean?" I ask nervously, wondering if he's going to put that needy mouth back on mine.

He tilts up my chin with a smolder that makes me want to drop my guard and smash my lips to his. When he'd done it yesterday at the airport, I was taken off guard and not prepared. Next time he does, I want to be ready.

"I see how much time and effort you put into being a mom and how busy you are with the store. So...what do you do that's just for yourself?"

Is this where I tell him I use a bullet vibrator in the tub until I orgasm three times and then pass out for seven hours?

Yeah...I'm not admitting *that*.

"Between Serena and the shop, there's not much time for

anything else." I shrug. "When I tried datin' after the divorce, it got too hard balancin' it all. So I just stopped lookin'."

"I have no doubts you've been the most amazin' mother, but I wish you'd take some time to do something just for you. That way, you don't burn out tryin' to do it all."

"My mom and Howie were very helpful whenever I needed it," I explain, hoping to use this as an opening to tell him the truth about his best friend.

"Well, I'm here now. Let me do something for you." He holds out his hand, and I skeptically give him mine.

"What're you doin'?" I ask as he leads me out of the kitchen.

"You'll see."

He walks us into the master bathroom, and I gasp when I see what he's done.

"Ayden..."

The lights are off, but candles are spread around on the vanity and counters, giving just enough dim lighting to see he drew me a bubble bath.

"What's this?" I ask in disbelief. "When did you do this?"

"Earlier when you were on the phone with your mom. I've not been able to take care of you for ten years. When I found your candles and bubble bath stuff, I decided you deserved a break and some time to yourself. I'll clean up the kitchen and do whatever else needs to be done. As long as you promise to relax in this tub for at least an hour."

Opening my mouth, I shoot my gaze to his. He wraps a hand around my neck and pulls me into his chest when I try to argue. My palms flatten against him as my breath hitches. His eyes never leave mine as the corner of his lips tilts up in amusement, his mouth torturously close to mine.

"I found your little toy under the sink and thought you might wanna use it, so I placed it on a stack of towels next to the tub for you." His low voice sends shivers down my spine, and then the reality of his words smacks me in my face.

Oh my God. I'm mortified.

Then he kisses my forehead and walks away, shutting the door behind him.

I don't claim to be perfect, but when I slipped into the hot water and looked at the bullet he so nicely set out for me, I folded. I won't admit it to him, though.

He'll just have to use his imagination if I did or not.

But goddamn, I'd never made myself come so many times in a row before.

That kiss, the sentiment of what he'd done for me, the teasing.

My body exploded.

Once I dry off and tie on my robe, I walk into my bedroom, fully expecting to see him waiting for me there.

What I get is so much better.

"What is this?"

"Thought you'd like some dessert after your *orgasmic* bath."

"Ayden Carson, that's not funny..." My cheeks heat as a blush crawls down my neck.

"You don't like peach cobbler?" He raises a brow, knowing damn well that's not what I'm talking about.

"You know I do. How'd you get that anyway?"

"There's this fancy little delivery app y'all have here..."

Laughing, I sit on the bed next to him with our dessert between us. "Y'all don't have that on the ranch, I suppose?"

"Not unless Mrs. Hollis counts."

I snicker, taking the fork when he hands it over. Then I take a bite and moan.

"Good, huh?"

"So good," I hum. "I haven't had this in ages."

"It's all yours, darlin'. Wanna Coke with that?" He stands.

"Wait, you aren't havin' some? I don't mind sharin'."

"I wanted to spoil you." He leans down, brushing his nose against mine. "So just enjoy it." The low drawl of his voice nearly has me begging him to kiss me again. Touch me. Anything to put me out of my misery.

Instead, I swallow hard and nod. "Thanks. I'll just take some sweet tea."

"You got it." Then he kisses my forehead and goes to the kitchen.

Jesus. My forehead's gotten more action in two days than the rest of my body has in a decade.

He texted me every night since I visited the ranch—some sweet and some dirty. Now he's here, dangling his charm and hotness in my face but not giving in to what we both want.

He's going to make me fucking beg, isn't he?

Well, I won't. *Yet.*

Not until I've told him the truth about Howie and our past.

But goddamn, do I want to break my rules for just one more kiss.

Telling him tonight would ruin everything he's done for me, so for now, I'll wait.

We made plans to go to Howie's grave tomorrow, and I'll tell him then.

I just hope he forgives me once I do.

Chapter Nine

Ayden

I've been dreading this day for weeks, but I need to do this.

Say goodbye to Howie Adams, my childhood best friend.

The man who was there for Laney when I wasn't, who knew my daughter before I did, and one who didn't deserve to die so young.

Serena said she wants to cook supper with me tonight and that it'd cheer me up once we got back from the cemetery.

It's the only thing holding me together. After drawing a bath and ordering dessert for Laney last night, I wrote him a letter while I waited for her to get done. I poured my heart into it, knowing I'd struggle to say those words to him today.

"Ya ready?" Laney asks in her bedroom doorway, looking stunning as usual. Her golden blond hair is down, feathered around her shoulders, and her green eyes meet mine.

Once I finish putting on my shoes, I stand and blow out a breath. "Yeah. Let's go."

Serena skips down the hallway as Laney takes my hand and squeezes. I know this is hard on her, too. She called me after the funeral and cried. She held it in for the sake of Howie's family and Serena. But when we spoke on the phone that night, I told her it was safe to release her grief. I hated that I couldn't be there to hold her as she cried. Howie was a really good friend and helped out a lot with Serena. Losing him caused a big hole in her heart. I feel even worse knowing her support system is gone, and I wasn't back soon enough to thank him.

During the drive, Serena rambles about when Howie dressed up as a hippo at her last birthday party. She cracks up at the memory of Howie letting her friends hit him with a plastic baseball bat until he gave them candy.

I shoot my gaze to Laney, brow furrowed in a *what the fuck* expression. She bursts out laughing and shrugs.

"He loved kids."

I know he wasn't married, but I never asked about kids. "Did he have any?"

She shakes her head.

"Uncle Howie couldn't get married," Serena tells me. I hadn't realized she was listening.

Narrowing my eyes, I turn around to face her in the back seat. "How come?"

"Because we're in the Bible Belt!"

"I...I'm missin' something." I turn to Laney, her face pale as she focuses on the road.

"Um..." Laney clears her throat, but Serena speaks up before she can continue.

"Uncle Howie and Uncle Reagan weren't allowed to be married," Serena states. "But they had a vows ceremony."

"Who's Reagan?" I ask Laney.

"His partner," she tells me.

"Howie was gay?"

She nods. "He came out to his family five years ago. But I knew long before then."

I blink, shocked that Howie never told me and that Laney didn't either.

"Why didn't you tell me?"

"I was gonna."

"That's why Howie moved out. He wanted to live with Uncle Reagan instead," Serena adds.

"He lived with you?" *Why the hell didn't she tell me that, either?*

"Yeah, for a while..."

"What aren't you tellin' me?"

She pulls into the cemetery and quickly glances at me. "Can we talk about this later?"

"Sure, but we *will* be talkin' about it..."

I loved Howie like a brother and wouldn't have cared either way if he was gay, but why wouldn't she share these details with me after talking for the past few weeks?

Once she parks, she grabs the bouquet of roses we picked up earlier and leads me to his plot. His stone isn't set in yet, but a variety of flower arrangements are around it. I kneel, rubbing a hand over the fresh dirt and grass.

"Hey, buddy..." I manage to choke out. God, I wished I'd seen him at least once more before he died. How goddamn unfair.

"Uncle Howie, I got to meet my daddy finally!" Serena gushes, and a new wave of guilt and emotions floods my veins. "He's a *rancher* now." She giggles.

I laugh at the unexpected admission she tells him.

"He'd find that funny too," I admit with a grin. A football star turned ranch hand.

Pulling out my folded letter from my pocket, I tuck it into

the roses and place it next to a set of dying ones. "Read that when you get a minute," I murmur.

"What's that?" Serena asks.

"Just a little thing I wrote him."

"Can I read it?"

"Serena Mae. *Manners*," Laney interrupts.

Serena frowns.

"Sorry, kiddo. It's adult stuff."

"I know a lot about adult stuff," she exclaims.

"I know you do, baby, but it's personal and for Uncle Howie only," Laney explains.

Serena furrows her brow at being left out. "I'll write him my own letter, then."

"That's a good idea." Laney smirks.

"I'll give you the CliffsNotes," I tell Serena.

"The what?" Her upper lip curls in confusion, and Laney and I both laugh at her not understanding the reference.

"I told him how awesome it was to finally meet my daughter and how cool you are," I say, standing and giving her a side hug.

"Well, obviously," she singsongs.

"And I told him how you and your mama are as pretty as a peach," I continue.

"You did?"

Smiling, I nod and steal a glance at Laney's expression. Her cheeks are tinted pink.

"Ever since I was thirteen, I thought your mama was the most stunnin' woman I'd ever seen." She stole my heart, and I never wanted it back. "And we have a beautiful little girl."

"I saw photos of Mama when she was younger wearin' braces and glasses." Serena snickers.

"Hey, don't make fun." Laney scowls.

"And she was the prettiest four-eyes there ever was," I taunt.

Laney playfully smacks my arm.

I hope Howie's looking down at us, smiling and laughing.

After another few minutes, Laney takes Serena's hand and says she'll give me some privacy. Kneeling, I blow out a breath and try to find words to express my gratitude. "I owe ya one, Howie. I should've been a better friend and contacted you when I settled. I'm sorry I didn't. I was a scared kid." I go on and on about ranch life and thank him repeatedly for taking care of Serena and Laney when I wasn't here to do it.

"I wish I knew about Reagan sooner. Maybe I'll meet him before I go."

After a few more minutes, I decide it's time to return to the car. Laney and Serena are jamming out to country music, and hearing them sing makes me smile.

"You okay?" Laney asks once I settle in my seat.

The grin on my face is sincere. "Never been better."

Chapter Ten

Laney

Watching Ayden sit at Howie's grave shattered my heart.

He doesn't know the full truth, and the longer I wait, the more hurt he'll be. I can see the guilt in his eyes, and I know it'll only cause more.

Though I did try again last night.

We devoured my infamous homemade pizza, watched a movie, and snuggled on the couch. Serena passed out between us halfway through. After Ayden carried and tucked her into bed, I asked if he still wanted to talk.

He hesitated, like he wasn't sure if it was the right time. He was tired—emotionally and physically—and we decided it was better to talk when we were both clearheaded.

I know he's confused about why I didn't tell him about Reagan, but things were so messy with his family that I didn't want to bring him more bad news. Howie's dad was a father figure to Ayden, and knowing what happened once Howie came out will destroy Ayden. He'd wish even more that he'd been here for him.

But I can't protect him forever.

He needs to hear it all.

"Mornin'," Ayden greets as he walks into the kitchen with messy brown hair, shirtless, and sweats hanging low on his hips.

"How'd you sleep?" I ask, fighting the urge to stare.

"Great. Your bed is damn comfy. You sure you don't miss it?" The taunting tone in his voice has me wanting to play his little game, but Serena's sitting at the table, so I don't.

"Coffee?" I ask instead.

"Yes, please."

He grabs a mug, and I pour him some.

"What's on the agenda today, ladies?"

"Shoppin'!" Serena squeals.

"Where're we goin'?"

"The boutique. My mom wants to see you," I tell him.

He gulps down his sip. "Oh. Why do I feel nervous like she's about to whip my butt into next year?"

I chuckle, remembering the first time Mama caught us alone in my room. She nearly chased him out with a wooden spoon.

"Serena's been talkin' about you nonstop, so she's excited to see ya."

"Should I wear a cup?" he whispers.

"I think you're in the clear. She already knows we had sex and made a baby," I whisper back.

"I heard that," Serena announces, and my eyes widen.

"No, you didn't," I retort, hoping I'm right.

"Were you and Daddy married when I was born?"

"No, sweetie. We weren't," I tell her honestly.

"Oh. I better call Meemaw then."

My brow furrows at the mention of my grandmother. "Why?"

"To tell her she's wrong. She said couples had to be married

85

to have babies, but if you two weren't married, then she's wrong." She shrugs innocently.

Jesus Christ. I need to listen in on their phone calls more often.

Ayden stares at me wide-eyed above the brim of his cup as if he's glad to stay out of this conversation.

"Perhaps you and Daddy can talk about that tonight," I tell her, shooting a mischievous grin in Ayden's direction.

"Um..." He blinks at me.

I pat his shoulder. "Tappin' you in, *Daddy.*"

It's a gorgeous sunny day out as we walk downtown. Serena skips ahead of Ayden and me as our hands brush. Neither of us has mentioned the kiss from the other day or how hot and bothered he purposely makes me when he inches closer to kiss my forehead. After he put Serena to bed, he pulled me into a tight hug and thanked me for taking him to Howie's grave. Then his breath lingered on my cheek as if he were fighting the urge. I was frozen in place, too scared to get rejected, so I just waited.

When he finally moved, I felt his mouth on top of my head as he exhaled and told me good night.

I was tempted to sneak into my own bed and demand he touch me, but we both needed sleep.

Today's day four of his visit, and he'll be flying back to Tennessee in three days. We never talked about us being a couple again, only when we could visit so he could see Serena.

But I swear I'll combust if he doesn't kiss me again before he leaves.

I know it leaves too much up in the air for what it'll mean for our future, but I've missed him so much that I don't care about the consequences. Of course I want us to be a family, but we live nine hundred miles apart, so one of us would have to move.

"Here we are," I say when the sign *Bless Your Heart Boutique* comes into view.

"Wow...it's changed so much," he says when we stand in front of the doors.

"Wait till you see the inside."

Serena opens the door, and a blast of cold air hits us in the face.

"This looks completely different." He glances around. "This is impressive, Lane."

"Thank you." I smile wide because I'm proud of how far it's come. "We expanded our Southern sayings on T-shirts to other items like mugs, tumblers, journals, phone cases, and much more. The tourists love it."

"Nana!" Serena shouts once my mother comes over.

"Ladybug!" They collide for a hug as Ayden and I approach.

"Hey, Mom."

"Hi, sweetie. Ayden."

"Miss Bennett. It's lovely to see you."

"You look so grown up," she says as her gaze moves up and down his muscular body.

"He's a rancher!" Serena blurts out, and I swear, she's told everyone who'll listen.

"I heard. He must be big and strong to do that, huh?" My mom smirks.

"I went from scrawny to brawny," Ayden taunts, getting a giggle out of Serena.

"I'm gonna show him 'round," I tell Mom, then grab Ayden's hand.

"She hates me," he whispers in my ear as we make our way to the other side of the store.

"No, she doesn't."

He cocks a brow in disbelief. "I'm sure she's not liked me very much the past several years."

"She was madder than a wet hen when I told her I was pregnant and you were long gone. But was shocked I'd found you and that you agreed to come visit. As long as her granddaughter is happy, so is she."

He blows out a breath. "Is she gonna be upset when you bring Serena up to see me?"

"She's already told me to take some time off to do that, so she supports the two of you buildin' a relationship. I think she's just a little weary, is all. Doesn't want Serena to get hurt."

Or me.

"Neither do I," he admits softly.

We change the subject as I show him the most recent items I've added to the store. More local crafters and unique jewelry not found on major online retailers.

"I love it, Lane. I see so much of your style in here." He points at the T-shirt that reads *Classy, Sassy, and a little Badassy*.

I snort. "Thanks, I tried to incorporate other little things but wanted to brand the shop and give it a special niche to make people wanna come back."

"Don't let her modesty fool ya for one second," Mama says

from behind, and we both turn. "She's been busy as a cat on a hot tin roof."

Ayden chuckles. "I believe it. Laney was always a hard worker."

"That she is. So what'd ya think, Ayden? Like it?"

"I love it, Miss Bennett. You two should be proud."

"Thanks. We are." She smiles sincerely before a customer drags her away.

"Serena, it's time to go," I call out when the doors open. One of the part-time workers starts helping as customers flock inside.

"But, Mom..."

"Serena Mae..." I warn.

"Yes, ma'am."

She heads toward the exit, and I quickly wave goodbye to my mom.

As soon as I step out onto the sidewalk, Mr. Hendersen spots me and nods at me. "Ms. Adams. Hot as Hades out here, ain't it?"

My heart drops into my stomach as I force out a quick response and continue walking with Ayden by my side. Serena's ahead, deciding where she wants to go next.

"Why'd he call you Ms. *Adams*?"

That's Howie's last name.

Swallowing hard, I walk to the edge of the sidewalk so we don't block anyone.

"He forgets that's not my last name anymore."

He takes off his ball cap and scrubs a hand through his hair. "I'm gonna need more than that."

"I was gonna tell ya."

"Tell me what?" He quirks a brow.

"Howie and I were married."

He steps back. "You married my *gay* best friend?"

"Ayden, listen..." I move toward him. "It's not what you think. We had an arrangement."

He folds his arms over his chest, keeping his gaze on me. "What kinda arrangement?"

"His family would stop meddlin' in his love life and"—I brace myself for the words I have to force out of my mouth— "your dad threatened to take Serena if I couldn't prove I could support her on my own. Gettin' married killed two birds with one stone."

He comes closer, his shoulders high and tense. "My father *threatened* you? What'd he do?"

"Mom! Dad! Are y'all comin'?" Serena shouts, but we continue staring at each other.

"Let's talk about this at home, okay?" I tilt my head toward Serena, who's waiting on us.

"Fine. But we *will* be talkin' about it."

Fuck.

I was afraid of this. He won't be upset about Howie and me having a marriage arrangement but rather about what his father did. Ayden's bigger now, stronger, and older. He could easily hurt his dad if he wanted to and that's what scares me.

Mr. Carson would get Ayden arrested in a heartbeat if he touched him.

Chapter Eleven
Ayden

I can barely think straight as we pull into the driveway. Serena's bouncing in the back seat with a sugar high as she talks about a boy named Sawyer Beck. We saw his family at the ice cream parlor, and apparently, the kids had a spat in school a few months ago. Laney assured me she handled it, which I have no doubt she did, but I was ready to tell that little boy to keep his hands off or it'd be the last time he used them.

Being a girl dad suddenly brings out a rage I thought was only fueled by my parents. Turns out it's also brought on by little nine-year-old boys who dare to push my daughter and make her bleed.

My anger wouldn't be so high if it weren't for what Laney told me. Howie's secret life, him having a partner, helping with my daughter, and now, husband to my high school girlfriend.

Though I'm not mad about them being married.

I'm upset they *had* to.

And enraged my father threatened her and she didn't tell me about it sooner.

I didn't plan to see him while I was here—fucking prayed I

wouldn't — but there's a sudden urge to change that. He deserves some payback for the black eyes and broken ribs he gave me.

Once we're inside, Serena takes her shopping bags to her room and starts organizing the new things I bought her. Laney said I shouldn't spoil her, but I can't help it. I have nine years' worth of spoiling to do. If my daughter wants it, her daddy's getting it for her.

"Ayden?" Laney murmurs in the doorway of her bedroom as I sit on the mattress.

"I need a moment," I tell her honestly. My brain is still playing catch-up.

After a minute of silence, she speaks up. "I loved Howie as my closest friend. Nothin' more."

"I'm not upset about that, Lane." Tilting my head, I meet her gaze. "You came to me over three weeks ago and told me I had a daughter. Then you neglected to tell me details about the lives you three shared after sayin' you wanted me here. You said you were gonna tell me, but then why didn't ya? Why keep it a secret?"

She frowns, inching closer. "I did try a couple times. We either got interrupted or I chickened out. I was scared I'd lose you again."

Her soft, nervous voice has me furrowing my brow, and I stand. "Why would you think that?"

"If I'd told you those things — that your father threatened me, and Howie and I were married for five years — I was scared you wouldn't want this. *Us.* I didn't know what to expect or how you'd act when I saw you for the first time in ten years. I worried all this baggage upfront would be too much to handle. Your dad's the reason you left in the first place. I thought anything involvin' him would make you pause at comin' here."

She takes a deep breath, her eyes downcast as she bites her lower lip. "So I waited to tell you because I selfishly wanted you here. I wanted you to meet our daughter and show you the possibility of what we could have. As a family."

The pain in her voice has me closing the gap between us, and when I tilt up her chin, tears fall down her cheeks.

"I'm sorry you felt like you couldn't tell me, Laney. I'll do whatever it takes to rebuild that trust so you know that I'll be here for you and Serena no matter what. I don't care how big or small. If it involves either of you, I wanna know. I'm not goin' anywhere. I promise."

"I'm sorry. You deserved to know sooner."

I cup her face, wiping away her tears with my thumb. Unable to resist, I lean in and softly press my lips to hers.

Slow and hesitant, she moves her tongue with mine, and I tease her mouth with mine. Tasting, giving, taking. I want to claim her.

Laney Bennett has always been mine, even miles apart and a decade later.

She always will be.

"Please tell me what my father did to you..." I murmur, pulling back just enough to lean my forehead against hers. My thoughts immediately go to what he did to Gabby, and I'll kill him if he touched Laney. I've seen him do shady shit my entire life, so he'll pay for whatever he's done.

She nods. We sit on the bed and face each other.

"A few months after I found out I was pregnant, your dad came to the store while I was working and asked if what he heard about me was true. I pretended not to know what he was talkin' about, but he could see my little baby bump and said he'd be takin' me to court for full custody."

"Full custody? That's fuckin' crazy."

"He proclaimed I wasn't fit to be a mother or to give a child what they needed without a father. I was too young, and since I was raised by a single mother who then got knocked up at eighteen, there was no way he'd let his only grandchild be raised by a single mom, too."

"That bastard," I mutter, shaking my head. "Shoulda told him to go fuck himself."

"I wanted to. Mama was so mad when I told her, but a family lawyer friend said he'd have no grounds for gettin' custody and not to worry."

"But my father isn't just anyone..." I say, knowing where this is leading.

"Exactly. A couple months later, I received a letter from a judge sayin' if I couldn't prove sufficient stable income or a spouse with insurance, Mr. Carson would become the legal guardian on behalf of his son...*you*."

"There's no goddamn way." I shake my head in disbelief. "In what world is that possible?"

"Accordin' to the lawyer, if a judge signs it, then it is."

My father has so many connections and dirt on everyone from being a lawyer, it shouldn't surprise me that he'd find a way to use that to get what he wants. He's a dirty authority leader and always has been.

"How'd the conversation of you and Howie gettin' hitched happen?"

"Mama told me she'd spend every penny she had payin' a lawyer to fight this, but I didn't want her to lose the store. I knew your father would win if it came down to goin' to court, so when I asked the lawyer what my best option was, she suggested findin' a husband. Someone who had a job and health insurance so Mr. Carson had no claims to his case."

"Christ." I shake my head at the thought of how I'm the one

who put her in that position in the first place. It's my fault. I'm the one who left. Of course my father would shove his nose where it didn't belong. He always inserted himself into places he had no business being in.

"I told Howie, and he suggested *we* get married. We were already friends, but I couldn't see how it would benefit him. Then he told me his grandmother and aunts were pressurin' him to get married and settle down with some kids. I had a gut feelin' why he didn't want that, but when he emphasized that his religious Southern family would never accept him, a former football player, for who he was, I knew."

"Wow, I can't believe he'd rather hide than just tell them."

"You know how it is down here, Ayden. Similar to the stigma of being a young, single mom out of wedlock. People judgin' all the time."

"Yeah, I do know." I was expected to follow in my dad's footsteps, play college football, graduate from his alma mater, settle down with a family, and then start a political career. Doing anything outside of that would be frowned upon.

"Howie was workin' full time at his daddy's garage and makin' good money, so we knew it'd be enough to get the mayor off my back and his family's off his. So we got hitched, and he moved in with me at Mama's house until we bought a house a year later."

"Did you have plans for how long y'all would stay married?"

"Not really. We were good friends and happy being roommates since neither of us had any interest in datin', so it wasn't a pressin' issue. I figured once I was on my feet financially, there'd be no reason for your dad to come after me. It wasn't until he met Reagan that things shifted."

I blink, processing everything. "I can't believe Howie did all that."

"He loved you, Ayden. You were his childhood best friend, and he would've done anything for you. Anything to make sure Serena and I were protected. Includin' marryin' your baby mama in a courthouse when she was eight months pregnant and then helpin' with the baby." She releases a small, humorless laugh.

"I should've been here."

She shrugs. "Or I should've gone with you."

"How'd Howie's family take the news about Reagan and the divorce?"

"Not well at first. Especially his father and grandmother. Eventually, they came around and decided they loved Howie enough to understand he was with a man, whether or not they accepted it. They ended up lovin' him once they put their judgments to the side. His father even walked with him down the aisle at the vows ceremony. It was very sweet."

"Thank you for tellin' me, Laney. I want to know everythin', okay? No more hidin'. I'm not goin' anywhere." I lean my forehead against hers and fight the intense urge to taste her lips again.

"Ayden, there's one more thing…"

"Mommy! There's an old man at the door." Serena's voice has us breaking away before Laney can continue.

"Who could that be?" I ask Laney.

"I'm not sure. Probably a salesperson. They get a little ridiculous 'round here."

The weight of what Howie and Laney had to go through weighs heavily on my shoulders as we walk down the hallway. I wish I could've paid him back for what he'd done to protect my girls.

"Dad, can you get me some juice?" Serena asks me.

"Manners," Laney reminds her as she walks toward the door.

"Please," Serena immediately adds.

"Of course." I smile, then follow her into the kitchen. "What kind?"

"Grape! That's my favorite."

"One glass of grape juice comin' up," I singsong as she hops on a stool.

"What do you want? You can't be here." Laney's strained, hushed voice from the living room has me focusing on her conversation. "Go. *Now*."

"Who's that?" Serena asks.

That's a goddamn good question.

"Be right back. Stay here." My voice turns stern.

"I'm not leavin' until I—"

"Dad?" I ask when I see him across from Laney.

"See my son," he finishes.

"What're you doin' here?" I cross my arms, then firmly stand next to Laney.

"You didn't think my only son returnin' to town wouldn't make its way to me, did you? I had to see for myself." He straightens his tie and bores his eyes into mine.

"Well, here I am. Now you can leave."

The amused expression on his face makes me want to shove my fist in it.

"You're done playin' around in the hay fields, huh? Finally ready to be a dad and husband?" He crosses his arms, firmly planting his feet as if to say he's not going away that easy. He's used this intimidation tactic my entire childhood, but it no longer works on me.

I step closer, pulling Laney out of the way so I'm face-to-face with my piece of shit dad. "I know what you did. So take your schemin', lying self off Laney's porch and go drive into a ditch. You're the reason I left in the first place, and you know it."

"Don't blame me for your actions, son. If you truly loved her, you could've come back to check on her. Then you would've known much sooner that you had a child."

"Don't talk about my daughter. You're nothin' to her." My teeth grind so hard I feel a piece chip off in the back.

"Who are you?" Serena comes up next to me. I curse under my breath at her for not listening and staying put in the kitchen. Laney tries to intervene, but it's too late.

My dad kneels with a conniving smile. "I'm your grandfather."

"Go," I tell him harshly. "You're not welcome here."

Serena pulls on my shirt. "Why not?"

Swallowing hard, I tell her the truth. "Because he's the reason I left."

My father clears his throat. "I'm the reason she lives in this house and goes to an elite private school."

Laney gently takes Serena's hand. "Go to your room, sweetie. I'll be right there."

"But, Mom—"

Laney gives her a firm look. Serena nods and then walks away. Once I hear her feet echo in the hallway, I turn toward Laney.

"What's he talkin' about?"

"She didn't tell ya?" My father's amused voice is followed by a chuckle.

"I was just about to," Laney whispers. "Before he showed up."

"How convenient." He laughs. "While you were busy playin' rancher boy, I was here—supportin' your child."

"You mean the one you threatened to take from her mother..." I hiss.

This makes no sense. Why would he try to get custody and then give her money for Serena?

Control.

If he couldn't take her, then he'd play puppet master instead.

"How much?" I ask Laney.

She blinks. "What?"

"How much has my father given you? I'm gonna pay him back every penny so he has nothin' to hold over us. So...how much has he paid over the years?"

"I don't know..." she murmurs, shaking her head.

My father chuckles devilishly. "Well, let's start with the house. Fifty thousand for a down payment. Even with a fake husband, you didn't think a twenty-year-old single mom with a part-time income could buy her own house, did you?"

"What else?" I ask firmly, ignoring the urge to bash his head into the door.

"Four years of private school at ten thousand a year."

Another forty.

"Keep goin'," I say, adding it up in my head.

"Twenty thousand in supplies, clothing, and private tutors. Sixty thousand for her SUV."

"That it?" I keep my lips in a firm line, not wanting to give him the satisfaction of how pissed off I am.

"Pretty much. We'll call the rest gifts from her grandfather."

"Great, I'll send ya a check. Don't come near me or my girls again. I'll be the only one to support my family from now on. Not that you ever knew how to be a part of one."

"You can't afford their lifestyles from workin' up in Tennessee shovelin' horse shit. You should be grateful, son. I'm the reason they didn't end up homeless or eatin' out of a dumpster. They live in a nice, safe neighborhood. I've kept them protected."

In exchange for what? My father does nothing for free.

Narrowing my eyes, I keep my feet glued to the floor so I don't do something stupid that'll get me thrown in jail. Knowing my father, he'd press assault charges the moment I touched him.

"I'll be *grateful* the day I get to bury you six feet under and spit on your grave," I tell him, then step back and slam the door in his face.

"Ayden, that's a hundred and seventy thousand dollars."

"I know." I walk to the kitchen, grab the empty glass on the counter, and fill it with juice for Serena.

"You don't need to pay him back. He gave me that money because he felt guilty knowin' he's the reason you left in the first place. He's just tryin' to ruffle feathers now that you're back."

I slam the jug of grape juice down. "I do not want to give my father any leverage over me. He didn't do it because he felt guilty. He did it because it was his way of controllin' the situation."

"What're you talkin' about?" She folds her arms, leaning against the counter.

"As soon as news broke out you were pregnant with my child, *his grandchild*, he wasn't about to let the community see you struggle. That'd reflect badly on his reputation. His reelection campaign. It was to save *his* ass, not yours. He doesn't give a shit about either one of you."

It's why Serena didn't know who he was. If he truly cared, he would've asked to meet her years ago.

"I'm sorry, Ayden. I was about to tell you. Truthfully, I did need that money. I hated that I did, but I figured as long as he wasn't harassin' me with custody papers or asking to see her, it wasn't hurtin' anything."

I take the glass and walk it to Serena's room, then softly knock on her door. "It's me."

She opens it with a frown. "Can I come out now?"

"Here's your juice." I hand it to her.

"Daddy and I need to talk, sweetie. Put a movie on, and we'll get you shortly for supper."

"Fine," she mutters, then takes a sip of her drink and closes the door.

"If you're insistent on payin' him back, then at least let me help. I make enough money. Plus, I'm gettin' a portion of Howie's inheritance. I didn't need your dad's money once the store took off, but he kept insistin'. Tellin' me to send her to the best schools, hire top-notch tutors, and make sure she had nice clothes for church. I started savin' some of it in an account for her."

"You're not usin' a cent of your money to pay him back," I tell her with finality.

"Ayden, please..." She follows me to her bedroom.

"Laney, I said no." I turn around, and she bumps into me.

"Stop bein' stubborn." She puts her hands on her hips, brow furrowed.

"My father knew where I was, Laney. He knew and didn't bother to tell me I had a daughter. He continued to throw money at you and keep his reputation shiny and clear. So no, you won't give him a damn thing. I have savings from years of workin', never buyin' anything new, and keepin' it for a rainy day. I'll pay him back for what he provided, so I never owe him a damn thing again. You need anything for Serena, you ask me.

She needs money for school, I'll pay the tuition. Let me be her father and support her now, okay?"

She steps back with a confused brow. "How do you know he knew where you were?"

"Because he said up in Tennessee and mocked me for workin' on a horse ranch."

"Someone could've told him? Serena's been tellin' everyone who'll listen that her daddy's a rancher," she reminds me.

"Trust me, I could see it in his face and hear it in his voice. I don't know how he found me or why he didn't do anything once he did, but everything he does is calculated and precise. He knew as long as I stayed away, he could keep his reputation clean. Lettin' me stay gone was his way to prevent me from runnin' my mouth about what he did to Gabby. He knew I wouldn't stay quiet forever."

Although he could only run for two terms as mayor, he still had his prestigious law firm. A scandal as big as knocking up a high school girl and then forcing her to get an abortion would not only ruin his reputation and family, it could put him behind bars.

"I'm sorry, Ayden. I wish I hadn't taken a dime from him. But I was scared and worried he'd do something bad if I didn't accept it."

"It's not your fault, Lane. I'm not mad at you." I hold her close, rubbing my hands up and down her arms. "I'm gonna pay him back and kick him out of our lives for good."

The worst part of this revelation? He could've told me I had a child years ago and didn't. Just like he's done my entire life, he chose himself.

While I thought I was hiding from him in fear, he knew where I was all along.

Come With Me

And I hate that I spent years away in fear of him.
The bastard was going to pay.

Chapter Twelve
Laney

"Why did that man come here?" Serena asks when I go into her room. She's watching a movie and sitting on her bed.

I take a seat next to her. "Because he wanted to see Daddy."

"Is he bad?"

Licking my lips, I contemplate how to answer. Though I don't want her to be afraid, she's too young to fully understand.

"He's not a nice man," I choose to tell her. "He and Daddy don't get along."

"How come?"

Ayden clears his throat before walking in and kneeling beside us. "Because he used to hurt me and my mom. I left so he couldn't touch me again or ruin my life. Turns out, I should've stayed and stood up to him."

"Why didn't you?" Serena asks. She's always been a curious little girl.

"I was scared. He holds a lot of power, and I was just a kid with none. I thought startin' over somewhere else would keep me safe."

"But then you didn't know about me."

Ayden's lips tilt up in a small grin. "You're right. I wish I had known."

"Would you have stayed?"

"Absolutely!" He meets my eyes because we've already had this discussion. "I would've married your mama and given you a few siblings."

I blink and swallow hard.

That we did not discuss.

"Well, it's not too late!" she exclaims, bouncing on the bed. "I'd be a good big sister now. My friend Maisie has two little brothers, and she helps her mom all the time. She even gives them baths!"

Ayden flashes me a smirk, and I swear my cheeks turn a hundred degrees hotter.

"I like that idea," Ayden says.

I nearly choke on my tongue trying to spit out the right words. "Um...who's hungry for supper?"

"Me! Can we have tacos?" Serena asks.

"Sure, sweetie." I stand, then kiss the top of her head.

As I walk out, I glance over my shoulder and watch Ayden. He says something to make her laugh, and it's the sweetest thing I've ever seen. I'd love to have more babies with him, but we have a long way to go before we have that conversation.

Once I'm in the kitchen, I open the fridge doors and stand as close as I can, letting the cool air hit my flushed skin.

This man has kissed me, twice now, and him mentioning knocking me up is what has me losing my damn mind.

Blowing out some breaths, I steady myself and gather the ingredients needed. After everything's on the counter, I get the meat on the stove and start cooking.

The steam blows in my face, and when I put on the fan, I feel two steady hands on my hips and jump.

"Jesus, you scared me."

"Guess you didn't hear me walkin' in," he murmurs against my ear and slides his tongue along the skin underneath. "What's on that mind of yours?"

Before I can respond, he brushes my hair off to one side of my shoulders and rubs the length of his nose over my exposed neck.

I'm nearly panting by the time I find my words. "Ayden, what are you doin'?"

"Watchin' you cook."

With his chest flush against my back, I have no room to move except to stir the meat.

"And to ask if you needed any help," he adds with a hint of amusement.

His mouth finds the perfect spot on my neck, and he sucks lightly, sliding his tongue around as he holds me in place. My chest rises and falls as I try not to react and fail miserably.

"Better watch what you're doin' so you don't burn yourself," he warns when the water boils to the top and inches back to give me space. Quickly, I reach over and turn down the burner.

"You're distractin' me," I counter, inhaling harshly as I feel his erection press into my lower back.

"Then you better focus..." His taunting voice echoes as his hand moves between my thighs. My breath hitches as he rubs his palm over my center and creates friction between my jean shorts and his hand.

"Ayden..." I fight to keep my eyes open. "I can't when you're doin' *that*."

"Should I stop?" He chuckles before feathering kisses down

my neck and adding pressure to my clit. He knows exactly what he's doing.

"Um..." My head nearly falls back to his shoulder.

"Or should I keep goin'? Your pussy's so wet, I can feel it through the fabric."

Oh God, that's embarrassing.

"Tell me what you want, Laney. I'm not doin' anything without your permission."

I bite my lip while trying to stay focused on not overcooking the meat. Ayden's teasing has me so worked up, my head spins as I undo the button of my shorts and lower the zipper.

"Touch me," I plead, somehow controlling my breathing so I can speak. The meat's done, and I need to add in the seasoning, but it will have to wait.

Ayden slips his hand beneath my panties and groans when he slides down my slit. "Fuckin' hell, baby. You're drenched."

"You better hurry before we get interrupted," I warn.

His bemused chuckle vibrates against my ear. "Think you can keep it down?"

God, I hope so.

Nodding, I spread my legs wider for him.

Ayden coats his fingers before thrusting inside me, the intrusion harsh and delicious, and I nearly collapse on the stovetop. His free hand wraps around my waist, holding me in place as he continues his assault, driving faster and harder into me.

"Holy hell, you're tight."

"It feels so good."

He twists his wrist, and as he sinks in deeper, I gasp at the intrusion. My head falls back as I lean against his chest and cling to him for support.

"Shit, I'm so close," I whisper, and moments later, my body shakes as I try to hold back a scream. He covers his mouth with mine as I moan through the sensation.

"I don't know what spot that was, but goddamn, you found it," I say once my vision clears.

He chuckles lowly before sucking on a sensitive spot between my neck and shoulder.

As he slides out of me, he brushes against my clit, causing me to shiver.

"I didn't bring any condoms with me, so if you sneak into my bed tonight, just know I fully intend to come inside you. Take that warnin' and decide if that's what you want." Ayden's deep voice is followed by him licking his fingers and shooting me a wink as he walks away.

Wait. *What the hell did he just say?*

My brain's in a fog as I finish dinner and while we eat. Serena talks our ears off, and Ayden uses the opportunity to slide his hand under the table and squeeze my thigh.

Glancing over, I watch as he focuses on Serena and rubs his fingers between my legs. When I trap his hand, he flashes me a dirty little smirk and rubs harder.

I look at Serena when we finish the ice cream sandwiches we had for dessert. "It's bath night, and by the looks of your messy face, you need one."

She giggles as she licks ice cream off her arm.

Ayden cleans up while I get her situated in the bathroom. She yawns, and I know she'll pass out as soon as she's ready for bed.

"Your taco was delicious," Ayden says as I walk into the kitchen.

My brows rise. "You had more than one."

"Oh, I wasn't talkin' about the food, though they were tasty, too."

"Ayden Carson, you better stop flirtin' with me." I blush, walking around him to get to the fridge.

He wraps an arm around my waist and yanks my back to his chest, burying his face in my hair. "Are you still pretendin' you don't want this?"

"I never said that," I argue because I definitely do.

"Then why are you fightin' it, baby?"

I gulp at how that one word of endearment brings me back to when I was a teenager, and it'd make me all tingly inside. I felt special.

Like I was his whole world.

"You leave in a few days," I remind him as his hand slides up and cups my breast.

"I know. Doesn't mean I won't see you again. We'll take turns visitin' each other."

"And how long can we do that before we're tired of it? What about when Serena goes to school?"

Ayden spins me around to face him, then tilts up my chin.

"I don't have an answer for that, but I'll do whatever it takes to see you and Serena as much as I can. Until then, we'll figure it out."

Even though I want to beg him to stay, to give us a chance to make it work here and be a family, I nod. He loves his job, and the Hollises are his family, too.

"My mom texted earlier and said she hired a new manager. I'll be trainin' her for two weeks, and then Serena and I can come to see you."

"Yeah? That's great." He smiles wide, then dips his mouth to mine, brushing his lips softly against mine. "I should warn her I might not let you leave."

Chapter Thirteen
Ayden

It's two in the morning, and I can't sleep since I've been waiting for Laney to sneak her sexy ass in here. *Did I push her too far?* I tried to hold back and keep my distance, but it's nearly impossible around her. Laney's the only woman I've ever wanted, and when we're together, all I think about is kissing her.

Deciding to get up for a drink, I pull on my sweats and tiptoe to the kitchen. Lights from the fridge illuminate the room, and I find Laney leaning against the counter with a mug.

"Can't sleep?"

She jumps with wide eyes, and the liquid from her cup spills over.

"Sorry." I laugh, handing her a towel from the hanger.

She takes it and wipes her hands. "I'm not used to you being here and sneakin' up on me."

"What're you drinkin'?"

"Lavender tea. Want some?"

I scrunch my nose. "No, thanks. I'll just have water."

"Don't knock it till you try it."

I fill a glass and take a long sip. "How long you been out here?"

"Couple hours," she admits shyly, lowering her gaze down my bare chest and swallowing hard. "Tryin' to decide whether sneakin' into bed with you is a good idea."

Setting my glass on the counter, I walk over and stand in front of her. "What're the pros and cons? Maybe I can persuade you one way or the other."

She chuckles, meeting my gaze. "There's that charm again."

Grinning, I pull her into my arms and sigh happily at the familiarity of having her close.

"You're scared," I offer, and when she nods, I add, "I'll move here."

Her jaw drops open as she blinks up at me. "What? You can't—"

"I just did." I kiss the tip of her nose. "If us being hundreds of miles apart is makin' you stressed and anxious, then I'll fix it. I'll find a job here."

She licks her lips before pulling me in tighter. "I don't know what to say."

"Say that you're happy?"

Her laughter rattles our chests. "Beyond happy. I just hope you don't end up resentin' me later."

Leaning back, I cup her face and trace her bottom lip with my thumb. "You seem to have forgotten, Laney Bennett, you're the love of my life. My soulmate. My forever. I've never stopped lovin' you, sweetheart, and nothin' you could do or say would ever make me resent you."

She wraps her arms around my neck and draws our mouths together. Hot and urgent, our lips move in sync as I lift her up and set her on the counter, then stand between her parted legs.

Our hands roam each other, her arms lifting so I can remove

her shirt, and I'm greeted with bare perfect breasts. Trailing my mouth to her nipple, I suck it between my teeth. Her sweet moans echo above us as she leans back on her elbows and gives me easier access.

Laney's fingers thread through my hair as she holds me against her chest. I move to the other nipple and suck harder.

"Oh my God, that feels too good," she pants out each word as she spreads her legs wider.

My hands gravitate to her pajama pants. I lower them with her panties and let them fall to the floor.

"Fuck, Laney. Laid out for me like a Thanksgiving feast. I'm goin' to devour you, baby." I lick my lips, and she blushes in embarrassment.

"You did not just compare me to a dead turkey."

Chuckling darkly, I bring my mouth to her center and play with her needy clit.

"Don't be offended. That's my favorite holiday, and you just topped it." When I throw her thigh over my shoulder, she gasps at how deep my fingers thrust inside. She's so wet, and I've barely touched her.

"You're gonna come for me and let me taste you, sweetheart. Got it?" I blow warm air over her clit.

"I don't know if I can be quiet," she admits.

Serena's room is just down the hall, so she's gonna have to try.

Without another word, I fuse my mouth to her pussy, sucking and licking her clit as I maneuver my tongue up and down her slit. Laney can barely contain herself as I thrust my fingers deeper.

"Ayden, holy shit." Her whispered pleas fill me with pride as I edge her closer to the top. She squeezes my head with her thighs as she pulls my hair, begging for it.

As I continue my assault on her sweet cunt, Laney thrashes and pants as she struggles to keep herself in control.

"You're close. Now be a good girl and come on my face." I shove my thumb between her lips so she doesn't scream when I latch my mouth back to her clit.

"*Aye-ðin*," she mutters around my hand.

Her thighs shake, and the rest of her tightens as she arches against my face. Flattening my tongue against her pussy, I lick up to her clit and devour every drop.

"Good God," I growl, tasting my lips and pulling her toward me. "You're so fuckin' sweet."

She's still panting when I kiss her lips.

"You okay?"

"I've never come that hard in my life," she murmurs. "Not even with my bullet."

"Maybe next time we invite him to join us. He can be our little teammate."

"I'm not sure I could handle that," she admits, her cheeks tinted pink. "I should probably get dressed. This was risky with Serena in the house."

I grab her clothes and hate that she avoids my gaze while putting them on. Once she's done, I corner her against the cupboards.

"What's wrong?"

"Nothin'. I'm tired."

"Laney, talk to me."

"I'm fine, promise. I just wasn't expectin' that. At all."

She's overwhelmed, which I can understand, so I don't push her on it. "Okay. Do you wanna talk about it?"

"We can tomorrow," she insists.

I nod, then lead her down the hallway. "Well, you know

where I am if you change your mind and wanna chat." I squeeze her hand in mine.

She smirks and whispers, "Get some sleep. Serena wants to take you to a paintin' class at the Children's Museum, and it starts at ten."

"In the mornin'? Damn." I chuckle softly, realizing I'll probably get less than five hours of sleep by the time she wakes up. Without waiting for a response, I bring my mouth to hers and tenderly kiss her. "Sweet dreams, darlin'."

Chapter Fourteen
Laney

God, what is wrong with me?

As soon as Ayden gave me the most mind-blowing orgasm I've ever had, my head clouded with doubt.

What if we don't work out or he hates it here?

What if he blames me for being stuck in Texas and leaves again, breaking my heart for a second time?

His proclaiming his love for me has made everything so real. It's what I'd wanted all these years, but now that it's happened, I'm swarmed with anxiety.

Ayden being here is a dream come true and everything I've ever wanted, but I'm worried my lack of sexual experience will add to my insecurities and fears. It's been years since I've been intimate with a man, and even before the last time I was, it had been years before that with Ayden. He was my first and only up until my divorce. My mom pushed me to *go for it* and date again, but it was an awful experience.

As he had me on the counter, spread out like his favorite holiday feast, there was that lingering doubt that I wasn't as sexually experienced as I once was with him. We couldn't keep our hands off each other during our teens, but it was puppy love. We had no responsibilities and no one else to compare the other to. But now, nothing felt as intimate as when his head was between my thighs, and I was floating to heaven on an orgasmic wave. The aftershock of what we'd done hit me harder than I expected. It'd been years since I'd felt that kind of intimacy, and I mentally shut down. However, the last thing I want is for him to think I'm not attracted to him or share the same feelings. I just need to push through my self-doubt and go for what I truly want.

So when I hear Ayden get in the shower an hour before we have to leave, I decide to *go for it*. He leaves in two days, and even though he's already agreed to move here, I want to make it crystal clear that I'm in this for the long haul, too.

I strip off my clothes, inhale a deep breath, and open the bathroom door. Steam covers most of him through the glass door, but the outline of him is visible enough for me to see how good he looks.

When I open the door, Ayden blinks at me and slowly lowers his gaze down my naked body. Stepping in, I move under the warm water, then close the door behind me.

"Good mornin'," I say casually.

He scrubs a hand over his face, wiping water out of his eyes and hair, and smirks. "Mornin'."

"You don't mind if I join you, do ya?"

"Uh, not at all." He smiles wide as his eyes linger on my chest.

"You gonna stare at me the whole time or share the water?"

He wraps his arms around my waist and then pushes me to the wall. "Oh, I plan to do more than stare, baby."

Grabbing the back of his neck, I pull his mouth to mine and intertwine my tongue with his.

He abruptly breaks away. "Wait. What about Serena?"

"My mom took her to Arrow Café for donuts and will meet us at the museum."

"Good, then you don't have to be quiet this time." He yanks me up until my legs wrap around him.

Our mouths crash, and heat pools between my thighs as his erection pulses against me. Lifting my hips, I rock into him, telling him exactly what I want.

"Ayden..." I nearly beg when he doesn't help dull the ache.

He moves his kisses to my neck. "Are you sure, Laney? I was serious when I said I didn't have condoms."

"Yes, I'm positive. I want you."

He growls in my ear. "Say that again."

I reach down between us, grip his shaft, and stroke him. "I want you, Ayden. Fuck me, *please*."

"Such a *good girl* usin' her manners." The devious smirk on his face has me angling myself to position the tip of his cock against my pussy.

"Take what you want, baby," he demands.

Arching slightly, he greets me with a thrust and pushes inside. With a gasp, I take all of him as he holds me tighter. My heart races at the strong connection I've missed for so long.

"Holy fuck." He presses his forehead to mine, and I know he feels it too.

As Ayden pins me with his hips, the water cascades over us, and our breaths catch with each intense movement.

"I've missed this, Laney. I've missed you." He cups my breast and squeezes as his lips find mine.

Ayden's tender words have me reaching closer to the ledge and racing toward the high that's soon to take over my entire body. He has me feeling everything at once—desired, needed, *loved*. I've never felt anything this intense before.

"We've missed out on so much for so long," I breathe out, holding on to his shoulders as he increases the pace.

"I'm gonna make it up to you. I promise." His words dive deep into my chest.

"You already are," I reassure him. "You being back means more than I could've ever dreamed."

"I'm never leavin' you again. I want nothin' short of a lifetime with you."

I melt into him, pulling his mouth to mine and handing over my heart. It's his—hell, it always has been.

Ayden's gaze finds mine as I unravel around him. He moves his hand to my clit and adds pressure until I fall over the edge, moaning and screaming through the waves of pleasure.

"I'm gonna come. You want me to pull out?"

"No!" I say urgently. "I want all of you."

Ayden curses under his breath as if he's trying to hold back but then buries his face in my neck and releases a deep moan.

"Fuck, your tight pussy feels too good." He grunts, thrusting a few more times.

"My whole body feels like butter." I lean back against the shower tile. "And I still need to wash my hair."

His amused chuckle rings through the shower. "C'mon, I'll help ya with that."

Ayden carefully lowers me to my feet and then rinses us off. He grabs the soap and lathers it between his palms before gliding over my skin with his calloused hands. "Sorry, they're kinda rough."

"Trust me, I don't mind."

He smirks, focusing on every inch of my body.

"Do you wanna talk about what this means?" I ask nervously. We've only discussed future plans as being Serena's parents.

"No, nothin' to discuss."

I frown as my brow furrows in confusion. "Oh."

He takes the shampoo next, lathers it, then massages it into my hair. I wait impatiently as he finishes rinsing it out and again when he does it with the conditioner.

"Laney." His low, gravelly voice has my gaze meeting his. "There's nothin' to discuss because I'm never lettin' you go. I'm movin' here to be a family. Not only as a dad to Serena. I'm here for *us*, too."

A grin forms on my face. "Like...as my *boyfriend*?"

Ayden releases an amused laugh. "I guess we can say that — *for now*."

"Or would you rather use the infamous *baby daddy* term?"

He cups my chin, his mouth inches from mine. "Sweetheart, you call me whatever you please as long as you're still screamin' my name when I'm inside you."

I groan, my pussy clenching with desire at how much I want him. "We better get outta here before I beg you to fuck me again."

He presses his lips to mine, sliding his tongue in and taking over. His hands roam down to my ass, and he playfully smacks a cheek. "I'm gonna fuck you over and over, sweet Laney. Gonna fill you with my come and then fuck you again. This time, I'm gonna make sure I see you pregnant."

"Ayden!" I gasp at his filthy words, nearly losing my breath at how much I want him to take me.

He cups my throat, holding me in place as he teases a nipple with his free hand. "I warned ya. Once I had you, there was no goin' back."

"You can't talk about knockin' me up so casually. That's something we should plan for," I say, then moan at the sensation of him massaging my breast.

"Why? We didn't plan it last time."

I roll my eyes. "This is different."

"I promised Serena a sibling, didn't I?"

"That's not a legit reason to have another baby!"

"No?" His fingers drop down to my clit. "You didn't mind the risk when I went inside you bare."

"Well, that's because I was horny. I wasn't thinkin' straight."

He lowers his mouth to my neck. "Fine, let's discuss it then. Wanna have my baby?"

"Ayden, you can't just..." My words die as he sucks on the sensitive part below my ear. "Oh my God, stop that. I can't be reasonable when you do that."

"Then don't be."

The ache between my legs returns, and I squeeze them for relief. He notices and increases his pace. His dick pushes into my lower stomach, and goddammit, I want him inside me again.

"Yes or no, darlin'? We're on crunch time here."

"Do you really wanna have a baby with me?" I ask seriously. "Not just the act of makin' one but the late-night feedings, diaper changes, and lack of sleep? The pregnancy cravings, hormonal changes, and stress of havin' two kids? This isn't gonna be easy."

He cups my cheeks, staring intently into my eyes and looking sincere. "I want *everythin'* with you. The highs and lows. The ups and downs. The good and bad. I wanna be here for all of it. Whatever that is, just the three of us, or if we add more to our family, I'm ready for it. I'm here. I wanna give you everythin' you've ever wanted."

"I wanna give you that, also," I murmur.

He missed so much with Serena and is actively trying to make up for that, so I understand him wanting another one.

"Honestly, I want another one, too. I just don't wanna do it alone."

"If I had my way, you wouldn't have to lift a finger. I'm gonna take care of you no matter what."

My heart flutters at the thought of watching him with our baby. For years, I thought this was as good as my life would get. Then he flipped it around and showed me how much better it could be with him in it.

Smiling wide with certainty, I say, "Then let's do it. Maybe you already have, but if it happens, then it happens."

With a cocky smirk, he turns off the shower, then lifts me and carries me out the door.

"What're you doin'? Oh my God, don't fall." I hold on tighter as he grabs the towel.

Water drips off us as he walks to my bed.

He sets me down on the mattress and towers over me with a hand on each side of my body. "I'm not doin' this *if it happens, it happens* shit. If I have a mission, I'm fuckin' completin' it. No guesswork."

"Then you better make it fast, *Casanova*. We gotta leave soon."

"Don't you worry." He flashes a wink as he spreads my thighs and sinks inside me. "I've never failed to finish a mission."

By the time we get dressed, we have to rush out the door to make it to the class on time. Luckily, my mom set up a table for the four of us so all we have to do is sit and start painting. Ayden sneaks side glances each time he looks over his canvas. I try to stay focused on what I'm doing, but it's useless. My mind races with what happened between us and the potential of me getting pregnant. His promises are what I've always wished for, yet I'm second-guessing if Ayden moving here will truly make him happy. Leaving behind his home, job, and everything he's worked for over the past decade is a big change. I love that he wants us to be a family, but I also don't want him to give up his whole life.

The more I contemplate it, the more I wonder if *Serena* and *I* need a fresh start. This town has years' worth of memories with Howie, which I love, but it's also a reminder of Ayden's father and the puppet strings he pulled. Being here would put us in proximity to Mr. Carson and his conniving and manipulating ways. Ayden wanted to be far away from his family, and moving back only gives his dad access to him again.

Though I'd miss my mom and hate leaving the store behind, she'll be in good hands. I'll train the new manager and am only a phone call away to assist with anything they need.

I've made my decision before we leave the museum, but I want to talk to Serena first. This has to be something she wants too.

If she's on board, then we're moving to Tennessee.

Chapter Fifteen
Ayden

The next two days in Beaumont fly by with family-friendly activities and some *mom-and-dad-only* activities, and then I'm packing my bags to go home. I don't want to say goodbye to my girls, but I know it's temporary. They will fly up in a couple of weeks to see the ranch and help me pack. I'll give Garrett my two-week notice as soon as I'm back. Even though I hate disappointing him, he's a good man who understands family comes first.

Yesterday, I met Reagan, and we talked for hours over beers while we had a cookout. He's deep in grief, but meeting someone so close to Howie was nice. I shared many stories of Howie and me growing up, and Reagan shared details of their lives together. They were in the process of adoption when Howie passed, which made me feel even more horrible. At least he got to be in Serena's life and be with someone who made him happy.

"Can't I come with you now?" Serena pouts as she sits on Laney's bed, watching me pack my carry-on.

"You gotta wait for your mama, sweetheart. I work durin' the day, and you'd be home all alone."

"Nuh-uh. I'd help you work!"

"Ya know, that is a brilliant idea!"

"It is?" she squeals, her whole face lighting up like a Fourth of July firework.

"Yeah! We'll wake up at five to feed the horses, fill up their water buckets, and then bring them to the pastures. Once they're out, we'll shovel their poop and wheel it out, then lay more straw before bringing them back in."

"Wait...I can't do all that."

"Sure ya can. Mallory does, and she's only a couple years older than you."

"But she lives on a ranch. She's used to it!" She pouts, and I can't help the laughter that bursts out of me.

"I'll teach ya. You'll have biceps as big as mine before you know it."

"Are you scarin' our daughter?" Laney waltzes in with a smirk planted on her beautiful face.

"Just givin' her a little insight to livin' on a horse ranch. A lot of work is involved. It's not all fun 'n' games."

"But the website says it is..." She gives me a *duh* expression.

Laney snorts. "She's gotcha there, cowboy."

"Well, since I have to work, maybe it's best ya just wait to come with your mama. We'll do all kinds of fun stuff then."

Serena folds her arms. "Fine. I hope it comes fast."

I boop her nose and kiss the top of her forehead. "It will."

Since our shower, Laney and I have slept in her bed the past two nights, and I've already grown used to her sleeping next to me. I'll miss her and Serena like crazy. It makes my mornings when I find them in the kitchen as they make breakfast and coffee. I know it'll be different when we're all living together and rushing off to work or school, but I liked knowing I'm waking up to my family when I go to bed at night.

Things have been amazing between Laney and me. After Serena goes to bed and we make love, I hold her, and we talk for hours. I might be close to being sleep-deprived, but it's so damn worth it. We've discussed expanding our family and what life will be like when we're all together for good.

I've never wanted anything more.

After I zip up my suitcase, I motion to them that I'm ready.

"Before we go, we have a surprise for you." Laney smiles wide, then nods to Serena.

"What kinda surprise?" I raise a brow.

Serena takes my hand and leads me down the hallway with Laney behind us. Once we get to the living room, Laney stands in front of me.

"There's been a change of plans with you movin' here," Laney says, and my heart sinks.

My eyes twitch as I look at Serena and then back at Laney. Both are smiling.

"What do you mean?"

Laney opens the front door, and Serena pulls me to follow.

"What's goin' on—" It's then I see a FOR SALE sign in the front yard. "You're sellin' the house?"

"We're movin' to Tennessee!" Serena shouts, and I stare at them in disbelief.

"We decided a fresh start is what we all needed, and in order to put the past behind us for good, we wanna come with you. We can buy a new house and make it our own." Laney chews nervously on her bottom lip as I cup her cheek. "What do ya think?"

"I...what? How is this possible?" I blink hard, trying to form a coherent thought. "What about the store and Serena's school? I mean, I'd love for y'all to live with me in Sugarland Creek. But you have a life here already. Why the change of heart?"

"It wasn't just my happiness on the line, it's yours too, and I know how much you love workin' there and the Hollises. You selflessly offered to move here without question, and as much as I appreciate that, I should've considered what you were sacrificin'."

"Plus, you have horses there, and we don't," Serena adds.

"Yeah, it didn't take much to persuade her." Laney laughs, and so do I.

I pull them in for hugs, kissing the top of Serena's head and then planting my lips on Laney's. "This makes me the happiest man alive."

We pile in the car, and Laney tells me about her plans during the drive to the airport.

They'll spend the next two weeks packing the house and will fly up to Tennessee while a moving truck brings their stuff. With the money from the sale, we'll use it as a down payment on a new house for the three of us.

"What if we built our dream house?" I offer.

"That's a bit more complicated. We'd need a construction loan and somewhere to build, and I'm not sure—"

"I'll buy some land from Garrett. He's offered it to me once before, but I had no reason for it at the time. This way, we can design it exactly how we want and make sure we have extra bedrooms." I flash her a wink, and she blushes, knowing exactly what I'm referring to.

"I love that idea." She squeezes my hand. "They won't mind us livin' with you in the ranch hand quarters until then?"

"Nah. It's a two-bedroom, and it'll be plenty of room

temporarily. And then when school starts in a couple months, Serena can take the bus with Mallory."

"Yes!" she squeals from the back seat.

"What about a job? Do you think any place is hirin' in town?" Laney asks nervously. "Maybe something in sales?"

"I have an even better idea for ya." I smirk. "Dena's openin' a massive gift shop next to The Lodge this fall. She's gonna have tons of merch—clothing, drinkware, key chains, magnets. You know, all the stuff tourists love. She'll need a manager to run it. And I just might have the connections to help you get an interview..."

"Seriously? That'd be awesome if I could do something on the ranch!"

"Yep, and then we could meet for lunch, or I could swing by to give ya some sugar." I waggle my brows.

"Gross." Serena groans, and we burst out laughing.

Two days ago, we sat her down to tell her that we were *together* together. We wanted her to understand that when they came to the ranch, Mom and Dad would be sharing a room and what that meant as a whole. When Howie lived with them, his bedroom was what is Laney's office now, but they were strictly roommates. Although they were married and everyone referred to them as Mr. and Mrs., Serena didn't know the details behind that. Luckily, she was too young to understand most of it. So we wanted to be sure she understood her parents were an actual couple who would show affection and, hopefully someday soon, get married.

She'd never been around anything like that, so she made a gagging noise the first time she saw us kissing in the kitchen yesterday.

Now it's just fun making her squirm in disgust.

"Just wait till she asks where babies come from," Laney leans over and whispers.

"Um...you didn't have that talk with her yet?"

"No. She's never asked." She shrugs. "I figure the time would come when she got curious or learned it in health class."

I chuckle at her expression as if to say she'd rather do anything but have *that* talk.

"Mallory learned from Landen when she asked a bunch of questions about the breedin' operation, and he told her all about baby-makin'."

"Oh my God..." Laney drawls with wide eyes. "Guess we better get to her before Landen does."

Checking in the back seat, I see Serena with her nose in a book, hopefully not listening to a word we said.

"Maybe we should in a couple months when we tell her you're pregnant," I say, keeping my voice low.

"We don't know that I'm pregnant. It's too soon."

"My boys got the job done. Don't worry."

She rolls her eyes and smirks. I want to reach over and tell her how much I love her, that it means the world to me that they're moving to Tennessee, and how badly I want to give her everything she's ever wanted.

Her dream house.

A husband and another baby.

The perfect family dream.

I've made it clear she's the love of my life. My soulmate. She's yet to say those words to me, but I'll wait. When she's comfortable and ready, I know she will because actions speak louder than words.

When we get to the airport drop-off, we get out, and I grab my bags.

"I'll see you in two weeks, okay?" I give Serena a tight squeeze. "Be good for your mama."

"I will. Can we FaceTime?"

"Of course, sweetie. Every night," I promise. Then I kiss the top of her head, wishing for these next couple of weeks to go by fast.

"I'm gonna go crazy not seein' you for two weeks," I tell Laney, embracing her in my arms and burying my face in her hair, inhaling her sweet coconut shampoo.

"We've gone ten years," she reminds me, holding me close. "We can manage a little longer."

"God, I hope so. And you better be in my bed every night." I press my mouth to hers, sliding my tongue between her lips and wishing desperately I could take them with me now. "I love you."

"I'll be anywhere you are." She smiles as I lean my forehead to hers. Then I kiss her once more before grabbing my bags.

"Text me when you land." She climbs into the driver's seat and rolls down her window. "Or FaceTime when you get home."

"I'll do both." I shoot her a wink, then wave to Serena in the back seat.

Walking toward the entrance, I'm excited and nervous for this next chapter of my life, but I couldn't ask for anything more.

But then three loud honks echo, making me stop before walking through the sliding glass doors. I turn around and hear three more.

I. Love. You.

Laney stares at me through the windshield and mouths, "I love you, too."

I shouldn't run to her and hold up the drop-off line. I definitely shouldn't leave my bags in the middle of the walkway.

But that's exactly what I do.

Rushing back toward her car, I poke my head through the window and claim her mouth. She cups my face and kisses me with deep fervor. Tears slide down her cheeks, and I break apart enough to wipe them.

"I love you so much, Laney Bennett. I always have and always will."

"I love you, too. So much."

Music to my fucking ears.

Serena pops her head up from the back, giving us looks as if we're crazy.

"I love you too, kiddo. See y'all soon, okay?"

With one final kiss to Laney's lips, I pull away and head back to my luggage.

I can't wait to tell Dena and Garrett about our plans. Noah and Mallory, too.

But Wilder better stay the fuck away for real this time.

As I sit at my gate, I think about how I'll manage financially to pay back my dad, but then I think about all the shit he's done and how he doesn't deserve it. All his secrets and scandals. The control over my family and me. The way he always manipulated the situation to get what he wanted. The more I dwell on it, the more I realize I don't want to pay him off to leave us alone. I want *payback*. I want to hurt him in a way he can't ever come back from. I'll use the money to hire a lawyer and my own private security team and expose him instead. He isn't the only one who has connections. It's what he deserves after intentionally hurting everyone I love. Gabby deserves justice, and I'm going to make that finally happen.

The best part?

The bastard will never see it coming.

He thinks I'm a coward, but I'll prove I can act like a Carson just like him.

People are scared of him because he's wealthy and powerful, but I'm not.

Not anymore.

Chapter Sixteen
Laney

It's been twelve days since Ayden flew home, and I've missed him like crazy. Since I spend my days training and nights packing, I'm exhausted by the time nine rolls around. On the days Serena doesn't come to the store with me, my neighbor, Mrs. Johnston, watches her. Apparently, Serena blurted out everything that's happened, and now most of the town knows what's going on since Mrs. Johnston is the town gossip. Not that I even care anymore since we're moving in two days, but now rumors are spreading about Mr. Carson. Between that and Ayden's plan, I fear it's only a matter of time before he shows up again.

As I lie in the tub, I FaceTime Ayden since I couldn't earlier when he called Serena. Though we've texted throughout the day, it's not the same as seeing his face.

"Hello, my love." He smiles wide when he picks up.

"Hey." He looks like he just got out of the shower. "Bad time?"

"Are you kiddin'? I've been waitin' all day to see your face. What're ya doin'?"

"Soakin' my sore muscles. Being on my feet all day and then packin' after supper has me exhausted."

Today was my last day at the store since I need to finish packing tomorrow and then on Tuesday we fly out.

"I wish I were there to help, sweetheart. Let me hire a company to finish that for y'all. You have enough going on."

"I don't want strangers in my house when I'm not around. Plus, I'm donatin' stuff, so it's just a matter of me going through it all. It's just one more day. I can handle it."

"Fine, but we can buy new things for the house when it's time," he reassures me. "So only pack what's crucial. Give away the rest."

Ayden found out a week ago that Garrett's offer to sell him land for us to build on is still on the table. After I pack up my house, Mama's gonna help clean and stage it. Then once it sells, we'll have the down payment and can get the process started.

"I'm tryin'," I tell him. "Serena's already made a Pinterest board of how she wants her room decorated and paint colors. So she's only bringin' her essentials."

I love how excited she is. This is a big change for all of us, and though we're leaving behind the only place we've ever known, it's worth it for all of us to be happy.

"I already know our master suite is gonna have a huge tub for both of us."

"Oh yeah?" I ask. "You have plans for us in this tub?"

"You bet your sweet ass I do. Too bad I'm not there now to take care of ya."

"Hmm...what would you do if you were?"

"You got Mr. Bullet nearby?"

Laughing, I reach over to my towel stack and grab it. "Right here."

"Good. Turn it on and do what I say."

I arch a brow, intrigued by this side of him. Pressing the button, it vibrates to life. "Now what?"

"Spread your legs and put it on your clit."

I do as he says and immediately groan when I feel it.

"Imagine I'm playin' with your tits. Rollin' and bitin' your nipple between my lips."

"Mmm...yes." I close my eyes.

"How's it feel, baby?"

"So good."

"Slide your vibrator inside your tight pussy and use it like it's my cock."

"God. You're gonna make me drop my damn phone."

"No doin' that. I need to see your gorgeous face when you come. Now do it."

His deep, demanding drawl has me following orders without complaint. The bullet glides in with ease, and my breath hitches at the intrusion. Once I'm used to the feel of it, I slide it out and back in.

"That's my good girl. Keep goin'. Ride it hard and fast."

I do as he says repeatedly. My pussy squeezes as I increase my pace.

"I'm so close," I murmur, my eyes glossed over as I meet his gaze through the screen.

"Now put it on your clit, baby. I'm about to come watchin' you."

He angles the phone so I can see he's stroking himself. It feeds my desire even more, and as soon as I see pre-come on his tip, I explode. My body shakes as I ride the waves of pleasure and moan out his name.

"Fuck..." He grunts out his own release, and I open my eyes just in time to see him come all over his lower stomach.

Once I turn off the vibrator and set it aside, I slide deeper into the water and watch as he cleans himself.

"That was hot." He smirks.

"It was. I've never done that before."

"Me neither."

"Look at us, ten years later, and still discoverin' each other's firsts."

"That's because it's always only been you, darlin'. Just wait till you get here. Gonna fuck you on every surface of my house. Then when we move into our new house, gonna christen every room in that one, too."

My cheeks hurt from smiling. "You're too much."

Shooting me a wicked grin, he says, "Yeah, but you love me anyway."

"That I do."

As I finish up in the bath, he gives me a quick update on the PI he hired. Although I'm not sure how everything's going to pan out, I trust he knows what he's doing. I fully support whatever he needs to do to take down his dad. It's been a long time coming.

"Before I move there, you need to tell me one thing first," I say once I change into comfy sleep clothes.

Furrowing his brow, he asks, "What's that?"

"I need the story on you and Wilder."

He barks out a laugh as he gets comfy in bed. "You really need to hear that story, huh?"

"Yep, especially if I'm gonna see him all the time. I'd rather know than be kept wonderin'."

"It's not really a big thing, but Wilder made it into one. He's such a playboy, he can't handle the thought of another guy pickin' up chicks he's interested in. Except I wasn't interested. I just made him think it was like that."

I blink, more confused than I was before.

"Okay, start from the beginnin' because I understood none of that."

"A bunch of us ranch hands went out to a bar in town. Lots of tourists, single ladies were there, and he was tryin' to pick up these two blondes. They were clearly out of their minds blitzed but all he cared about was gettin' them to his place. Well, one of their friends who was much more sober asked if I'd take the girls back to their hotel because she was worried they'd try to drive. Since I'm a gentleman and didn't want Wilder takin' advantage, I agreed. Except as soon as I got the girls in my truck, they said they couldn't go back to their hotel because they were on some college dance trip, and if their coach saw them return that drunk, they'd get kicked off."

"Oh my God, how old were these girls?"

"Twenty-one." He shakes his head.

"Geez. Okay, go on..." I begin my skincare routine after I prop my phone up on the mirror.

"So I take the girls to my house and get them settled into the spare room. In the meantime, someone tells Wilder I took both girls home to sleep with them."

"And you didn't bother to clarify?"

"Nah. I wanted him to think he lost two girls—to me. The little shit is such a womanizer, he needed his ego knocked down a few points."

Chuckling, I continue washing my face. "So what happened when you saw him next?"

"Well, as luck would have it, the mornin' after—when the three of us walk out to my truck so I can take them back to their hotel—Wilder comes out of his place and sees us. So I make some crude gestures and shoot him a wink. Then I get the girls in my truck and flip him the bird once I drive off."

I shake my head as the scene he describes plays in my head like a movie. "Are y'all sixteen?"

"Hey, this is how Wilder plays. You either put him in his place and play along or get stepped on by his giant boots. Plus, it gave me some good cred on top of pissin' him off. Double win."

"Great, so now he thinks my boyfriend had a threesome, and he's gonna try to sleep with me to get even with you."

"Yep, which is why he's gonna be even more pissed when he finds out you and I are together and have a kid. As soon as he finds out you're back, he'll be on you like Chicken Pox."

"Damn. Good thing I'm vaccinated."

His head falls back as laughter erupts from his throat. "This is why I miss ya so damn much. Always sayin' funny shit to put me in a good mood."

"Be even funnier if you let me flirt with him back, and then you walk in and kiss me right in front of him."

"You don't know how badly I wanted to do that the first time he laid eyes on you. Then the second time when I walked into The Lodge, and he was all flirty, I wanted to carry you over my shoulder and stake my claim."

"Okay, caveman." I roll my eyes and snort. "I would've been so embarrassed and never shown my face again."

"That's a shame because you're too gorgeous to be hidin'."

"Hush up," I deadpan, and he bursts out laughing at my mud face mask.

"I mean it. Serena clearly takes after you. I hope our next baby does too."

"Or we could have a boy, and he could be just like you."

"Charmin' and good lookin', right?"

I chuckle, brushing out my hair before putting it into a braid. "Yeah, but also a sweet and carin' gentleman."

"He'd be the cutest little boy in a cowboy hat and boots. Then he'd grow up stealin' hearts left and right."

The corner of my lips tilts up as I picture the two of us having another baby to raise together. "You better hurry and knock me up."

His mouth drops open. "Excuse me. As you may recall, I tried a few times when I was there. My boys went where they were supposed to. The rest is up to your lady parts."

"*My lady parts*? Yeah, this is why I have to give Serena 'the talk.' Perhaps you should be there and get a lesson yourself."

His amused chuckle echoes through the room. "Oh, I know plenty about your body. I could draw a map usin' my tongue and with my eyes closed."

"You'll have to prove that."

"I will." He waggles his brows and then quickly furrows them. "Shit. Zane's callin' me. I'm gonna take it, then I'll text ya."

"Okay," I say as he hangs up.

Ayden hired a security team, and they've stayed parked outside my store while I work and at my house until nine. Zane's a big guy, one I wouldn't want to mess with, but he seems good at his job. Ayden wanted it as a precautionary while he's away and if I'm being honest, it's helped ease my concerns about Mr. Carson.

I'm exhausted, so when I crawl into bed and close my eyes, I pass out before I can wait up for his good night text.

Loud knocking has me jerking awake in the pitch-black room. Blinking a few times, I feel for my phone and see it's only been thirty minutes since I spoke to Ayden, but there are several messages and missed calls from him.

AYDEN

> Get out of the house. Don't go to your mom's.

AYDEN

> I booked y'all a room at the Twins Hotel.

AYDEN

> Once you get there, lock the door and don't open it for anyone.

AYDEN

> Laney, let me know you're getting these! This is urgent, baby.

AYDEN

> I'm sending Zane over. Call me as soon as you're in the car.

What is happening? I jump out of bed and look through the peephole of the front door, finding Zane standing on my porch. "What's goin' on?" I ask him as I open it.

"Mr. Carson got a tip about his warrant and now no one can find him. You need to leave, ma'am."

"As soon as I get my daughter."

Fuck, this isn't good.

Zane nods and waits while I rush to Serena's room. She's sound asleep, and I hate that I have to wake her.

"Serena, sweetheart." I shake her a little, and she startles awake. "Sorry, baby, we gotta leave."

"Where?"

"A hotel. I'll explain later, okay?"

She nods, and I pick her up. Next, I slide on my shoes and grab my phone. Then I meet Zane in the kitchen who has the door to the garage open for me.

Once I dig my keys out of my purse, I throw it over my shoulder. Zane walks out with us and locks up. I help Serena into the back seat and buckle her, and then get into the driver's side.

"I'll follow you to the hotel and make sure it's secure before I come back here," Zane tells me as I get situated in my seat.

"Thank you, Zane."

I press the button to open the garage door, then click on Ayden's name on my Bluetooth and reverse out of the garage. It rings twice before a loud boom rattles the car, and my ears ring at the sound of an explosion.

Then my vision goes white, and everything fades.

Chapter Seventeen
Ayden

THREE DAYS AGO

"You ready to do this?" my lawyer, Shane Braun, asks as he seals the envelope with hopefully enough evidence to put my father away for two lifetimes. "No going back once it's sent out."

"Yeah, this is overdue," I tell him, eager as hell to get these files to Judge Carmichael's office.

Thumb drives with phone audio recordings, video footage, flight tickets, Gabby's cell phone records, her medical records, and much more are being delivered by a courier.

"You know what this means when it comes out?"

It means my father's going to finally pay for abusing and killing Gabby.

It's payback for all the torment he caused me and for threatening Laney.

"Yes, sir."

Judge Boyd Carmichael is the judge who helped my dad threaten Laney with custody papers ten years ago.

Now, he'll be indebted to me.

Gabby—the seventeen-year-old girl my dad had an affair with—was Judge Carmichael's daughter.

After all these years, he deserves to know the truth about what happened.

Gabby and I had been classmates since kindergarten and were friends. To say I was shocked she was having an affair with my dad was an understatement. Whether she did it to rebel against her father's strict rules or because my piece of shit dad seduced her, I'm not sure. My gut feeling tells me it wasn't consensual. My father's a manipulator and could've easily blackmailed her about something or someone. Her dad being as powerful as he was could've been what my father used against her, but she never told me.

The first time I suspected something was when I saw my dad sitting in her car in the school parking lot. What the hell was a middle-aged man doing talking to a teenage girl? Not illegal but definitely inappropriate. I snapped a photo so I could ask Gabby about it later. I was worried he was doing something to her, but she'd reassured me it was for a school project. She was supposed to interview someone in a career she was interested in pursuing. She claimed she wanted to go into politics and even though I wanted to believe her, I worried something more was happening.

A week later, I saw her sneaking into my house late at night. When I checked the security footage, I noticed the camera in my dad's office was conveniently turned off. There was no way she was interviewing him for a school paper, and that was confirmed when I peeked in and found her bent over his desk. Gabby looked terrified as his hand covered her mouth. Before I could barge in and put a stop to it, one of my dad's guards grabbed my arm and yanked me away. He was twice my size, but even so, I tried to argue and fight out of his grip. He forced me back and then stood in front of my dad's office door, restricting access.

The next day, when I asked Gabby about it and if he was abusing or forcing her, she promised it wasn't like that. No matter what I said or how many times I offered to help, she claimed it was consensual.

As the weeks went on, she became more distant, quiet, and a shell of her previous self. I noticed multiple bruises on her arms. I continued to offer to go with her to the hospital or the police, but she'd get angry with me and tell me to mind my own business.

As someone who grew up being abused and manipulated by him, I recognized the signs.

She needed help, but she was ashamed and scared—just like I'd felt most of my life. The fear that no one will believe you and you'll get ostracized.

Gabby didn't deserve that.

I needed proof so that when she was ready to come forward, there was direct evidence.

The last thing I wanted to do was hurt Gabby or make things worse for her, but in order to prove statutory rape, I had to get them on film. The photos were suggestive, but they weren't enough to imply they were having sex. If Gabby wasn't comfortable coming forward herself, I had to make sure there was evidence of my father's crimes.

The longer their affair went on, the more reckless my dad became about where he'd meet up with her. At his office with the curtains wide open, in his car in the middle of the day, and in his bedroom when my mom was gone.

It's as if he wanted to get caught. Made my job easy in terms of getting what I needed.

As I captured videos and photos, I uploaded them to an online storage site and gave Howie access to it. I needed insurance that if something happened to me in the meantime, someone else could leak it, but I didn't want them on my phone. I only uploaded what I knew would be enough and disposed of the rest.

Though I had my reasons for staying quiet at the time, I wish I'd said something back then. But between the risk of humiliating my friend and my father being the mayor, I was scared about the repercussions for Gabby and me. I also knew no one would've prosecuted him. He would've claimed she came onto him or it was consensual, and made a deal to cover his ass. Considering what he must have had on the judge in the first place, I wasn't hopeful justice would be served. Worst-case scenario, he would've gotten a slap on the wrist, and my life would've been over for ratting him out.

It almost was when he randomly barged into my room one day and demanded I hand over my phone.

When I told him to fuck off, he pinned me to the wall and wrapped his fingers around my throat, demanding I give it to him. Something had set him off to believe I had something on him, but I wasn't about to give in. I thrashed against his hand as I fought for my life. I'd never seen him in that kind of rage before. My legs kicked out, but it didn't faze him. All it did was make his hold on me tighter. My vision blurred as he continued screaming. It wasn't until my mother barged in and smashed a glass vase over his head that I could finally breathe again.

It was the first and only time she defended me.

After that incident, he stayed away from me but tracked my every move.

I continued to keep an eye on Gabby and be there for her as

a friend as much as she'd let me. But then she revealed she was pregnant.

My dad's campaign was all about pro-life. He didn't trust her to get an abortion on her own, and he couldn't be the one to take her. So he flew them out to Mexico.

Before their flight, Gabby gave me all her records as proof in the event something happened. She knew all too well how powerful my dad was, and there was no running away. Between my father and her dad being a judge, she would've been found and returned within twenty-four hours. She promised to end the affair after the procedure, leave for college, and never return. Though I wanted to believe her, that she wasn't being used against her own free will, I wasn't sure if she'd ever tell me the full truth. All I knew was that she needed to escape this place.

I swore I'd leave too, but unlike Gabby, I was leaving behind the love of my life to escape my version of hell.

My father deserves more than humiliation and being ostracized. He deserves prosecution for his crimes and Gabby's death. I want the world to know what a sleazebag he is and what he did to a judge's daughter. A despicable man like him doesn't deserve to walk the streets a free man ever again.

And once they bring him in for questioning and arrest him, every news station in Texas will have the details on what he's being accused of. Because we aren't only sending this information to the judge. Once he's in custody, the video footage and audio recordings will be mailed to every news station in Texas.

Laney didn't know the details of Gabby's death, only that the affair was happening. I was too ashamed to tell her after she'd told me to tell the authorities.

The police worshipped my father and would've laughed in my face.

I hate that Gabby died before I could tell the world what my dad did to her.

When I went to Laney with my plan to finally expose him, I told her everything I hadn't before. Howie was the only other person who knew the full truth and had access to my account.

After Gabby came home from her forced abortion in Mexico, she got sick and was too embarrassed to go to the hospital. I begged her to, worried she had an infection or internal bleeding. She had both.

During her autopsy, it was discovered she'd had the procedure, but there were no local medical records to confirm. There was no evidence to prove she was involved with my dad since he used a burner phone, and they were discreet in their messages. My dad continued to live freely, pretending he knew nothing about Gabby Carmichael's death, and I lived in fear that he'd kill me if I ever spoke up.

ONE DAY AGO

"My inside sources tell me they're issuing his warrant first thing Monday mornin'," Shane tells me when I call him on my afternoon break.

That's in two days.

Laney and Serena move the following day, and I'll have my girls back with me safe and sound.

"Thank God. I wanna see him in handcuffs."

"Soon enough, I'm sure. Judge Carmichael wants justice, especially since the ten-year anniversary of her death was a few months ago. He's pushin' the district attorney to make this big. They're gonna make an example out of him."

"Fuck yes." This is better than I'd hoped.

"Why're they waitin' till Monday then? Can't they go after him now?"

"They need to verify all the evidence first, but it's solid enough to be movin' this fast, so be happy about that."

I blow out a breath. "Fine, you're right."

"I'm sure you'll see him in an orange jumpsuit soon enough." He cackles.

We've already talked about the potential of me being a key witness, and if that's what it takes to ensure my dad never goes free, I'll do it.

"I'd rather the last time I see him be in a coroner's office," I murmur. "Assumin' he doesn't try to take me down with him."

"Expert witnesses will prove the evidence is legit for the jury," he reassures me. "Assumin' it gets that far. No doubt the defense will cross-examine you pretty hard. I wouldn't be shocked if they try to make you the bad one for withholdin' evidence ten years ago. And if they do, we'll fight back and make a deal."

That scared kid from a decade ago who hesitated to do the right thing due to the possible consequences isn't fearing his father's wrath any longer. I won't let Gabby's memory be stained or her death be in vain.

"Well...I know a judge who owes me one." I shrug, and Shane snorts.

I know it won't be that easy. Things will get ugly, but I'll do whatever needs to be done to finish my father off for good.

Before we hang up, I tell him to keep me updated on anything new and keep watching my girls.

Then before I go back to work, I text Laney.

Come With Me

AYDEN

Warrant's being issued for him on Monday!

LANEY

Oh good! I'll finally be able to stop wearing my Don't Mess With a Southern Mama T-shirt and holding my pink pepper spray!

AYDEN

Har har. You better keep that close.

LANEY

You know I am. Though I don't see the point. He doesn't know the warrant's being issued for him to come here and retaliate. And I really don't think he'll stop in to shop either. I mean, pink isn't really his color.

AYDEN

That mouth of yours just earned you a couple spankings.

LANEY

Ooh...I can EARN them? Please, tell me more.

She sends a batting-eyelashes GIF as if to act all innocent and cute.

AYDEN

You just wait, woman. In three days, that ass is mine.

Then that little devil sends me a naughty picture of her boobs.

And now I'm going back to work with a hard-on.

PRESENT DAY

In less than twenty-four hours, my dad will get the shock of his life.

I'm only disappointed I won't be there to witness it.

I chatted with Serena after work, and Laney texted after dinner that she'd FaceTime me once she got Serena to bed. She's been working nonstop, and I hate that she wouldn't let me hire someone to help. Zane and his team are still following them since I can't be there, but it's been worth every penny to help my sanity and keep them safe. With my father lingering around, I'd rather not leave them unprotected if he chooses to show up again.

When I finally see Laney's face and hear her voice, my face lights up. She's beautiful as always. I love watching her in the tub and telling her what to do to make herself come for me. Makes me more anxious and excited not only to see her in person but propose to her and get married one day soon. I'm not wasting any more time than I have to before making her my wife.

In the middle of our call, Zane beeps through, and I tell Laney I gotta take it, so I'll text her later. I know she's exhausted anyway and needs to get some sleep.

"Hey, man, what's up?"

"Someone leaked the warrant details to your father."

"Are you kiddin'? How?"

"Someone in the department. I don't know who, but I sent Oliver to his house and office to see if his car was there, and it wasn't."

"Son of a bitch. Think he fled?"

"It's possible, but I'm worried he thinks you're still here."

"Are you at Laney's?"

"Yeah, I'm parked right out front, but it's downpourin'. I can't see much out of my window. Do you want me to go in?"

My heart races as I think about what to do. Before I left, I secured her doors with extra deadbolts and a security system, but that wouldn't stop a determined man from finding a way in if that was his mission.

"If my dad's on the loose and thinks I'm stayin' there, he'd go to extreme levels to get rid of me." I have no doubt about that.

"Do you want me to get an officer over here?"

"There's no time. I'm gonna call Laney and tell her to get out. Stay put and watch the perimeter. Book them a room at the Twins Hotel in the meantime."

"Got it."

We hang up, and I immediately call Laney. It rings and goes to voicemail. *What the hell?* We were just speaking five minutes ago.

I call three more times before sending her a text.

AYDEN

Get out of the house. Don't go to your mom's.

AYDEN

I booked y'all a room at the Twins Hotel.

AYDEN

Once you get there, lock the door and don't open it for anyone.

I call five more times before calling Zane again.

"Go knock on her door. She must've passed out. Tell her to grab Serena and go."

"I'm on it."

AYDEN

Laney, let me know you're getting these! This is urgent, baby.

AYDEN

I'm sending Zane over. Call me as soon as you're in the car.

I call her twice more before Zane sends me an update.

ZANE

She's grabbing Serena now. I'll follow her to the hotel and make sure she's secure, then come back and check things out here.

Relief hits me knowing they're on the move.

AYDEN

Thank you.

Then I anxiously wait for Laney to call.

After what feels like an eternity, my phone finally rings.

"Baby, are you—"

An explosion-like sound echoes in my ear and then abruptly cuts off.

The call ends.

Chapter Eighteen
Laney

As I peel my eyes open, my head throbs in pain. The sound of a machine clicking isn't helping, and just as I look around the white room, a blood pressure cuff squeezes my arm.

I hate these damn things.

"Ms. Bennett, you're awake." A soothing voice echoes as a nurse enters the room with a rolling computer cart and stands next to me.

"Am I? Or is this the afterlife?" I squint at the sunlight coming in through the window.

She smirks, shaking her head. "You're gonna be alright, don't worry. That boyfriend of yours, however...I finally kicked him out to get some fresh air."

"Ayden's here?" I wince as I try to move. "Where's Serena?"

"Broken rib," she tells me, fluffing a pillow near my side. "That little sweetie pie is just fine. She's with your mom in the waitin' room. Most likely talkin' the staff's ears off about how she's goin' to go live on a ranch and have a bunch of horses. She's already named six."

I try to laugh, but it hurts.

"What happened?"

"Airbag went off in your car when the bomb exploded and knocked your head right into the metal doorframe. You had your seat belt on, so when the airbag hit you, it smacked right into your chest. Hell, it did its job, but the car wasn't moving, so the impact crashed into your body. Thank the Lord above you didn't break your collarbone or jaw. Those usually require surgery. Could've been much worse, Ms. Bennett. A broken rib and a concussion are minor injuries compared to what could've happened. The explosion made the roof of your garage collapse. A rib could've punctured your lung. The whiplash could've fractured your skull. A guardian angel was lookin' over ya."

"Wait, what? The garage? What about Zane?"

"The security guy?" she inquires, and I nod. "I'm so sorry, miss. He didn't make it."

My eyes widen just as the door flies open, and Ayden bursts in. The nurse tells me she'll be back in a little while.

"Oh thank fuck. You're awake, baby." He grabs my hand and then cups my face. "How are you feelin'?"

Confused. Heartbroken. Scared.

I swallow hard, my throat dry and sore. "Serena's okay?"

"Fine, sweetheart. Little warrior barely got a bruise." Ayden brushes his thumb over my cheek and tucks loose strands of hair behind my ear. "She was buckled in the back seat, safe and sound."

I rolled my window down to talk to Zane and then...I heard it. *Boom*.

"The nurse says Zane didn't make it?" I suck in my bottom lip.

Ayden shakes his head, lowering his eyes. "A piece from the

ceiling fell and landed on top of his chest. His lungs collapsed, and the impact of the explosion made him lose consciousness. He wasn't breathing by the time the paramedics arrived. They worked on him for a half hour, but it was too late."

Tears surface and fall down my cheeks. I can't believe he's dead.

"How long ago?" I ask, unsure of how long I've been here.

Ayden carefully sits next to me on the bed. "Two days ago. You've been in and out because of the pain meds, and they've been monitoring your concussion. Swelling went down this mornin' and they decreased your meds so you'd wake up."

"Do you know what happened? There was a bomb?"

With his help, I manage to sit up and inhale a deep breath. My head is spinning, and not only because of the injury.

"It's still an ongoing investigation, but early preliminaries have said a bomb was planted in the livin' room. Most likely they were nearby to see that Zane was there, and when y'all were headin' out, they activated it."

"Your dad..."

"He has two warrants out—one for questioning in Gabby's case and the other in regard to the explosion. They found him on surveillance at a Home Depot four days ago."

"That's the last he's been seen?" That would've been Friday.

"Yeah, the day after Judge Carmichael would've received the file we sent him."

"Someone tipped him off," I murmur.

"Looks that way. Boyd isn't happy. The police department put out a wanted alert. Wherever he's hidin', they'll find him."

"How are they gonna link him to the bomb?"

"Don't worry about that, sweetheart. They have lots of ways."

How is he so calm knowing his dad is out there somewhere?

"What aren't you tellin' me?"

Serena rushes in ahead of my mom before Ayden can answer. "Mommy!"

Ayden stands to give her room so she can hug me. "Easy, baby," he tells her.

Serena gets as close as she can, and I kiss her cheek. We chat before the nurse comes in to check my vitals. Ayden watches, and I know he's keeping something from me.

Once the room has cleared and my mom takes Serena home for the night, Ayden sits next to me with a cup of soup. He's insisted on feeding me, and because it hurts to lift my arm, I let him.

"How is it?"

"Bland," I say honestly.

"Well, don't get too full. Green Jell-O is next." His mock amusement almost has me laughing.

I finish the soup and flavorless Jell-O, then Ayden fusses with my pillows until I tell him I'm comfortable. The truth is, my ribs hurt like hell. But not much can be done about that.

He lifts the blanket and removes my sock. "You want a foot massage?"

"Sure, and while you're doin' that, tell me the truth about what's goin' on."

He raises a brow as his thumb digs into the arch. "About what?"

"The explosion happened two days ago, and you don't seem the least bit concerned that the man who put me in here and killed Zane is out there somewhere."

His eyes lower as he stays silent.

"Why don't we have security now? Is someone watchin' my mom and Serena? Is there a guard out my door?"

"No."

"Ayden Carson, I swear to —"

"He's dead," he blurts out, and I blink. "Sweetheart, he's dead, and he'll never hurt us again."

Chapter Nineteen
Ayden

TWO DAYS AGO

After the call from Laney ends, I try again repeatedly, but it cuts out each time. Zane's phone does the same thing. *Fucking hell, this isn't good.*

I decide to reach out to Oliver. He was looking for my dad, so I know he's gotta be close by.

"Hey, I've checked—" He starts as soon as he picks up, but I cut him off.

"Go to Laney's. There was an explosion. I can't get ahold of either of them."

"Holy shit. I'm goin' now." The squealing of tires echoes through the phone.

"I'm packin' a bag and gettin' on the first flight to Houston. Whatever happened, my dad's involved. You find him, you hold him for me. Got it?"

"Yes, sir."

"Text me and keep me updated. I'll let ya know when I'm headin' down."

"Will do, sir."

Once we hang up, I race to the airport and send Garrett a message on my way.

My heart hammers for a solid three hours. The one hour it takes to get on the flight and the two it takes to fly there are the worst. When the plane lands in Houston, I read text updates from Oliver that Laney and Serena were taken to the hospital. Then as I drive to Beaumont, I call him.

"Zane didn't make it," Oliver tells me as I speed to the hospital.

My stomach sinks. "Fuck, man. I'm so goddamn sorry."

"I have your father. Found him behind the house on the ground. He must've been too close during the explosion, and it knocked him out."

"Is he alive?" I ask.

"Well, his heart's beatin' if that's what you're askin'. Broke his nose and knocked him out a few times for killin' my friend. Now what do you want me to do with him?"

"Keep him for a bit. I gotta make a couple calls, then I'll let ya know."

"Will do." He hangs up.

Next, I call my lawyer and give him an update.

"I heard. The whole town's buzzin' with rumors on what happened. I suspect your father."

"Yeah, Oliver has him. I'd like to deliver him to Judge Carmichael myself and let him decide what to do with him. Think you can arrange that?"

He's silent for a beat before he clears his throat. "It's almost four in the mornin'."

"I'm sure he's awake," I say dryly. There's no way he isn't with a killer on the loose after that explosion.

He huffs. "Yeah, gimme a few."

I should tell Oliver to take him to the police department, but something tells me Boyd wouldn't mind dealing with him behind closed doors. He's already *missing*, so whether he keeps him permanently missing or not will be up to him.

As soon as I arrive at the hospital, I rush inside, and Laney's mom and Serena greet me in the waiting room. I called on my way to the airport to tell Ms. Bennett what I'd heard, and she was one of the first people to arrive at the scene after they pulled Serena out of the car. They look exhausted.

"Daddy!"

"Oh, thank God." I swarm my little girl in a tight hug. "You okay?" Kneeling, I spin her around, checking for any injuries.

"I'm okay." She holds out her arms so I can check.

"Good. Where's your mama?" I ask

"Restin'," Ms. Bennett says, approaching behind Serena. "She's banged up, but she's a fighter."

"Will they let me see her?"

"I told the nurse you'd want to as soon as you arrived, and she said you could for a few minutes."

I kiss the top of Serena's head. "I'll be right back, sweetie."

"She has a concussion, and we gave her pain meds, so she'll be out for a while," the nurse tells me as she leads me to her room. "She's got some bruises but should fully recover in a couple months. Broken ribs have to heal on their own with rest and limited activity."

Fuck. I shake my head with anger.

The nurse taps my arm. "It could've been a lot worse. Someone was lookin' over them."

Howie.

"Thank you," I whisper.

She nods, then leaves.

I hold Laney's hand and kiss her knuckles. Then I press my lips to her forehead. "I love you, sweetheart."

A few more minutes pass before the nurse enters and tells me I can return during visiting hours. I give her my number and ask her to call if there are any updates or if she wakes up.

"You two should get some sleep," I tell Laney's mom.

"What about you, Daddy?" Serena asks.

"I'm gonna stay here in the family waitin' room until visitin' hours start. I won't be able to sleep anyway."

"I'll bring you some food when we return," Ms. Bennett says.

"Thank you."

I give Serena one more hug and kiss before they leave.

Once they're out the door, I call my lawyer again.

"Boyd wants us to bring him to his house," Shane tells me. "You sure about this?"

"Positive."

Oliver picks me up from the hospital, and we drive to Judge Carmichael's home outside of Beaumont as my father lies unconscious in the trunk.

"He's alive?" I confirm as Oliver drives us.

"Last I checked," he deadpans, his grip firm on the steering wheel.

"I'm sorry about Zane," I tell him again. "He was a good guy."

He nods but stays quiet.

As we approach the judge's house, it's eerily quiet and still. Trees line up the driveway to his two-story home.

"This place gives me the creeps," Oliver murmurs. "Like dead bodies are buried out here."

I snort. "If there aren't now, I have a feelin' there's about to be."

Boyd stands on his porch as we approach. He's in jeans and a black jacket, both hands covered in dark gloves. We get out of the car and meet him by the trunk.

"Let me see," he says lowly.

Oliver pops the trunk, and I stare down at the man who brought me into this world. A sad, pathetic man now covered in his own blood.

"You were never here, Ayden. Understood?" Judge Carmichael says.

"Crystal clear," I reply.

He nods before his gaze shoots to Oliver. "Leave him on the ground. I'll take care of the rest."

Oliver obliges, lifting my dad out of the trunk and not-so-carefully tossing him to the concrete. My father makes a disgruntled groan as he hits the pavement.

"Argh. Howie."

"What'd he just fuckin' say?" I ask.

Oliver shrugs.

"Say it again," I demand, kneeling closer to his face.

It must take every ounce of strength my father has to pull in a breath as he repeats himself. "At least...I got...*Howie*."

My blood boils as he says my best friend's name and the implication of his words.

"You had him killed," I murmur, swallowing hard. My words are painful as I spit each one out.

My father's eyes struggle to stay open as he goes silent.

"*Why?*" I shout, demanding answers. When he shakes his head, I stand and kick him in the ribs.

It's the first time I've touched him. And damn, does it feel better than I imagined.

"Rot in hell," I hiss, then spit on his frail body.

Oliver pulls me aside as if to make sure I don't go overboard.

"I owe ya one," Boyd says. "Off the record, of course."

"No, sir. I owe *you*." I give one final glance at the man who ruined my life.

"Time to leave," Oliver says, slamming the trunk closed.

I walk to the passenger's side. "Let's go."

Chapter Twenty
Ayden

TWO WEEKS LATER

The more I obsessed over my father's last words, the more frustrated I got. It wasn't until Laney reminded me that Howie became a paralegal and worked for another law firm in town that it started to make sense. My dad probably saw him numerous times over the years. Howie must've said or done something to make my father aware that he had some kind of evidence about Gabby. It's the only thing I can tie together that'd make him a threat to my dad.

And if it's true, my father's a worse monster than I thought, and I have no remorse for turning him over to Judge Carmichael.

I wasn't planning on telling Laney the details with my dad and Boyd, but she begged, and I couldn't lie. Mostly, I was worried she'd think differently of me or demand I tell the police, but she never did. She said it was my decision and supported whatever I'd done. I knew she deserved the truth so she no longer had to live in fear.

Laney's house is uninhabitable, which means she can't sell it. We hired a lawyer to fight with the insurance company so she can at least get a payout. Everything inside needs to be replaced, but now that they're living with me in Tennessee, they only needed the essentials.

Laney's still on restrictions to take it easy and hates every second of it. She thinks she's fine and then moans that she's in pain after a while. She's not used to being taken care of, but I'm back in her life to change that now.

Garrett let me take some time off, but I still show up in the early mornings to help with feeding, and then by midday, I head back to make the girls brunch.

Regardless of not being able to sell her house, I had enough savings left over after I paid the security team and my lawyer. So when Laney's resting, she looks at ideas to keep busy.

Now that it's August, Serena starts at her new school in only a couple of weeks. Mallory's really taken her under her wing and shown her around. I have no doubt she'll thrive here and can't wait to watch her grow. Every day, she goes off running with her and only returns when hungry or tired.

"Laney, I'm goin' to the Hollises to grab the mail. Want me to bring back some sweets?" I ask, grabbing my truck keys.

"Ooh yes. See if she has those little brownie peanut butter bars left from the other day. If not, then the raspberry cheesecake ones. Oh, and—"

"Do you wanna just come with me?" I smirk.

She playfully rolls her eyes. "Are you allowin' me outta the house?"

Bending down, I slide my hands under her knees and lift her off the couch. "Smart mouths get spankings, so I'd watch that if I were you."

"You wouldn't."

"Oh, I will. As soon as you're fully recovered. I've been keepin' track in my head. You won't be able to walk for a month."

"You already won't let me," she sasses.

"Because you're clumsy as hell. I don't need you breakin' another rib." The last time she walked out to the truck, she tripped on the sidewalk and nearly face-planted. If I hadn't been right there to catch her, she would've added a black eye and bruised face to her list of injuries.

Laney wraps her arms around my shoulders and holds on tight. "I think you just like takin' care of me."

I lean in and press my lips to hers. "For as long as I'm alive on God's green Earth, I always will."

When we arrive at the Hollises' house, she walks inside on her own. Dena's in the kitchen with Gramma Grace as usual, and their faces light up when they see us.

"Hey, you two. Take a seat. I'm serving lunch." Dena smiles wide.

Although we didn't come for that, I know Laney's hungry, so we do as she says and find a chair. Dena hands me a stack of mail from the past few weeks. As we chat about Serena, I flip through the envelopes and find one addressed to me from *my mother*.

My mother, who I haven't seen in over a decade, because

when I came home, she stayed hidden. I wasn't even sure she was still alive.

Curiosity gets the best of me, so I rip it open while Dena refills our sweet teas. Wilder and Waylon file in, and their rowdy asses echo throughout the house.

"Well, Miss Laney. Aren't you a sight for sore eyes?" Wilder gushes, taking the seat next to her. He's still bitter that Laney and I are a couple, but I'm secure enough now to let him flirt because the love of my life only has eyes for me.

"I swear, you get more charmin' each time I see you," Laney sweet-talks him, and he eats it right up.

I roll my eyes at their banter as I unfold the letter and then a check falls out.

Holding it up, I read my name and $500,000 next to it.

What the hell?

"What's that?" Laney asks.

"A letter and check from my mom..." I'm too stunned to read the words on the page.

"*Your mom?* Wow." Laney's just as surprised as I am. "What's it say?"

Blinking, I clear my vision and look at the handwritten letter.

Dear Ayden,

I know you'll never believe me, but I'm going to say it anyway. I love you, son. I always have. Even when it seemed I didn't. My life was never my own. I'm glad you left when you did because you didn't deserve the abuse your father put you through. I'm sorry I brought you into a world that was only determined to bring you down. I hope you, Laney, and Serena are safe now. Your father "missing" has been the greatest blessing. I know I have you to thank for it, even if you don't want to hear from me. No excuse could take back what I allowed to happen. I wish I had the nerve to leave him and take you with me when I had the chance.

That's all in the past now, and I can't change that, but I can give you something for your future. They won't declare your father dead for a long time, but this money I saved is yours. It won't fix what he broke, but perhaps it'll give you a start to the life you deserve.

I hope one day you'll forgive me for being the worst mother. The more he abused me, the more I abused alcohol to cope. I was hardly functioning on my own, let alone as a mother. Again, it's no excuse, but I hope you'll accept this gift. Build your family their dream home and get as many horses as Serena can ride. I loved walking past the store every weekend and seeing a glimpse of her through the windows. She looks so much like you.

For what it's worth, I love you, and I hope you have everything you could ever dream of.

Love, Mom

Everyone's staring at me by the time I look up. Tears coat my eyes.

"Well?" Laney raises her brows.

"It's a check for half a million dollars."

"*What?*" they all shriek at the same time.

"Have I ever said that I think of ya like a brother?" Wilder says.

Waylon elbows him. "Shut up."

I hand over the check and letter to Laney across from me. They all huddle around her to read the words I never expected to read.

After a few minutes of silence, Laney looks at me. "I can't believe this. She knows he's dead?"

"I think half the town presumes so," I admit.

"This is life-changin' money, Ayden." Dena grins. "Hope this doesn't mean y'all gonna leave us."

"Of course not, Mrs. Hollis. Just means Laney's engagement ring gets to be as big as she wants."

Laney's eyes widen, and I chuckle.

"Ayden!" she whisper-hisses. "We're buildin' a house. I don't need an extravagant ring."

I've talked nonstop about making her my wife. She knows it's coming, but she doesn't know when. I'll do my best to surprise her when it's time. I hope to take her up on Sunset Trail and get down on one knee—the same place I took her when she showed up here—and ask her to marry me.

Leaning back in my chair, I cross my arms. "I beg to differ. Gotta make sure all the men 'round here know you're mine." My eyes slide to Wilder, who's pretending to be clueless.

"Men like Wilder don't even know what an engagement ring is, so if that's your plan to scare him off, you're gonna need a picture book to explain when a woman's off-limits to him," Waylon rambles off, and we all laugh.

"I think he'll get the message when he sees Laney's round belly in a few months." I shoot her a wink, and she rolls her eyes at me.

"Stuff like that is how rumors get started, Ayden Carson," she scolds.

"Are y'all tryin'?" Dena beams.

"Only every goddamn night," Wilder mutters.

I shoot him a death glare.

"*What*? I can hear y'all from next door."

Laney's face goes beet red, but I can't help laughing. She's not been cleared for that kind of *activity*, but that hasn't stopped me from giving her multiple orgasms each night.

"What's everyone laughin' about?" Noah walks in, glancing

around. She's dirty from riding and is wearing a cowboy hat to cover her wild hair.

"Clearly *you*," Wilder teases, noticing her appearance.

"Oh, quiet. I rolled off Donut durin' a stunt." She brushes dirt off her shirt.

"Noah, I swear that horse is gonna kill you," I tell her. Donut's her show horse, and she likes to practice on him before working on the others, but he's not always cooperative.

"It's not my fault! Donut wouldn't have spooked if Landen would stop ridin' his stupid dirt bike near the trainin' center."

"*What?*" Landen shouts, and a door slamming echoes throughout the house. "Don't be pointin' your finger at me. You were already on the ground when I walked in."

He comes into view, and Noah glares at him. "That's because the sound of it scared him before you came inside."

"You're wrong."

"No! You saw me fall! I know you did."

"What I saw was you moanin' and rollin' 'round on the dirt," he exaggerates his words, and it further pisses off Noah.

"Both of you, knock it off," Dena snaps. "Landen, no more ridin' your dirt bike near the trainin' center or corrals. Noah, you need a spotter if you're gonna do tricks like that. I've no interest in findin' you with a broken neck."

"Geez, Mama," Noah groans, sitting down. "I don't need a spotter. As long as no one spooks him, I'll be fine."

Dena's lips turn into a firm line not even I'd argue with.

Noah sighs. "Fine."

"Alright," Landen agrees.

"Wonderful." Dena claps her hands. "Now, who's ready for dessert?"

Epilogue
Laney

THREE MONTHS LATER

Mmm. My eyes squeeze tight as pleasure explodes between my thighs and shoots up my spine. I love it when Ayden wakes me up with his mouth on my clit and his fingers inside me.

"Louder, baby. You know Wilder likes hearin' you."

His amused tone has me smacking his head.

"Not funny," I murmur, spreading my legs wider. Thank goodness Serena spent the night with Mallory or we'd have to be quiet like normal. We definitely weren't last night.

As he flattens his tongue over my pussy, he thrusts faster until a shiver rolls through me. I teeter on the edge as he blows air over my clit, causing me to moan out in desperation.

"You gonna come for me, darlin'?" His tongue circles over me, slow and teasing.

"Don't stop. I'm so close," I beg, arching my hips to meet his greedy mouth.

Just as the buildup surfaces, Ayden's phone on the nightstand rings.

"*No*," I whine, the unexpected sound causing me to lose my orgasm.

"Shit, it's Garrett," he mutters, reaching over to grab it.

"Don't you dare—"

"Hey, boss. What's up?"

He fucking answered it.

Ayden smirks at my pouty face, positioning the phone against his ear and shoulder. Then he kneels between my thighs again and flicks my clit.

What the hell is he doing?

"No, it's fine. I'm just havin' breakfast." He shoots me a wink, and I furiously shake my head.

"Don't you dare!" I whisper-hiss, wiggling away.

He grabs my hip and keeps me pinned down on the bed. With his eyes fixated on mine, he shoves two fingers inside, and I gasp.

"Yeah, sure. Gimme twenty to finish eatin' and clean up. Then I'll meet ya out there."

Ayden continues finger-fucking me as I try desperately to hold back from making any noise. He makes it nearly impossible when his thumb adds pressure on my clit, and I cover my mouth with my hand to silence my moans.

I could easily get out of his hold if I wanted to, but he owes me an orgasm, and I'm not letting him leave until he gives me one.

"Sounds good. See ya soon."

When he finally hangs up, he tosses the phone and twists his wrist to fill me deeper. "Scream for me, Laney. I want my face covered in your pussy juices so I can taste it all day while I'm gone."

And that does it for me.

Ayden's filthy mouth has only gotten dirtier since we were teenagers. He worships my body like I'm his favorite painting and it's the only one of its kind.

"Oh my God, that was intense," I breathe out, panting my way through each word. "I can't believe you answered your phone."

He licks his lips, then cleans off the two fingers that were deep inside me.

"I wasn't about to let my boss get in the way of my favorite part of the day."

I roll my eyes, swinging my legs off the bed.

"Wait. There's a new tradition I want to start."

He carefully pulls me back down on the mattress and speaks to my stomach. "And good mornin' to you too, little one. Don't mind your mama's screams. She likes it. I promise."

Grinning, I shake my head at his ridiculousness. My heart squeezes at how excited he is already. We only found out two days ago when I took five pregnancy tests to be sure, but I already can't wait to see him holding our newborn.

Ayden kisses above my belly button, then trails his mouth up to my breast and sucks on a nipple.

"Fuck, I wish we had time to finish this, but Garrett's expecting me at the barn. New border today and they came early."

"Damn. Guess you'll just have to make it up to me tonight."

His mouth crashes down on mine. "I will, *future Mrs. Carson*. And every night after that as long as I live."

My heart flutters every time he calls me that. Ayden's the only man I've ever loved and the only one I will until I die.

When he suggested we take a hike a few weeks ago, I was finally feeling better but wasn't sure how far I'd be able to walk.

Then he told me we were gonna ride up there, which I hadn't done yet since moving here. I was excited, especially since I hadn't been on a horse in years. Not since I was little when my mom and Meemaw took me to a riding stable. But then, he surprised me with a picnic setup off Sunset Trail, the same one he'd taken me to the first time. I already thought this was a sweet romantic gesture, but then after we ate, he got down on one knee and gave me the surprise of a lifetime. He held out a much-too-big engagement ring, and of course, I said *yes*.

We celebrated that evening with a big party at The Lodge with food and drinks. I had no idea what was going on until I walked in, and they shouted *surprise!* I teased him about being presumptuous about my answer to plan a surprise engagement party ahead of time. Of course he knew what my answer would be. I loved every minute of showing off my gorgeous new ring and gushing about finally tying the knot.

Ayden asked my mom for permission—as if he needed it— but he wanted to include her. He didn't want Serena to be left out, so he bought a little promise ring to say he'd always be here.

Now that I'm pregnant, we've decided to elope and then plan a big reception for next summer after the baby is born.

I can't wait to tell Serena she'll finally be a big sister. When my mom visits for Thanksgiving in a few weeks, we'll tell her and everyone else.

I watch as Ayden gets dressed, appreciating how sexy the tight Wrangler jeans and work boots look on him. Now I wish we had time to finish what he started.

"Don't forget we're meetin' the contractors at four for a house update," I tell him. Once we signed the loan and contracts, we started building our dream house. They estimated it'd take five months, but it's on schedule to be done in four.

"I'll be there."

After getting ready, he gives me one last kiss and then flies out the door.

Instead of taking a shower, I soak in the bathtub before I have to go to work for a few hours. Dena's gift shop opened just in time for Halloween last month, and it's been a huge success. It's open to the public seven days a week, and the guests love it. Even those who aren't staying at the retreat are stopping in to visit. It took a couple of months for my ribs to heal fully, and they did right on time for me to start training.

When I get out of the tub, I stare at my naked body in the mirror and rub a hand over my belly. I'm probably only five or six weeks along, but I can't wait for my stomach to grow. Ayden missed out on so much the first time, as did I without him, so I can't wait to experience this pregnancy as a family now.

Once I get dressed and ready for the day, I text Dena to check on Serena.

She isn't back home yet, and I have a feeling she won't be until this evening. She's obsessed with the ranch and spends her weekends with Mallory and Noah. She loves watching them train, and in between, they give her riding lessons. At first, it made me nervous as hell, but she's getting the hang of it and is good at listening to their instructions.

DENA

> The girls ate breakfast an hour ago, then ran off with Noah. They wanted to watch her do some tricks on Donut.

I thank her for the update, then do some housework before driving to the gift shop. Since my car got damaged in the explosion, I was able to get a new SUV that'll fit all of us, including a car seat.

"Hey, Laney," Tripp greets when I walk in. He must've swung by after doing cabin call at the receptionist's desk, or he's filling in for someone.

"How's it goin'?" I ask.

"Steady, as usual. I swung by to help with the rush, but now that you're here, I can take off."

I walk behind the checkout counter and toss my bag underneath. "Feel free to stay. Unload some boxes, do some inventory."

He gives me a deadpan expression, and I laugh at his lack of amusement.

I flash him a smile, hoping he'll stick around at least through the rush. He rolls his eyes, finally agreeing.

As I ring up customers, he wraps the glassware and bags everything. Tripp's only a couple of years older than Noah and also trains horses, but he has a lot of random responsibilities on the ranch. I know he's probably needed elsewhere, so once the line dies down, I tell him he can go.

"I'll do this last one for ya," he says.

A woman who looks entirely out of her element with a large sun hat and sunglasses approaches. Her dark hair surrounds her face, and I notice her large designer bag and jacket.

"How can I help you?" I ask in my best customer service tone.

"Hello, Laney," she says, then removes her sunglasses, and that's when I recognize her.

Holy shit.

Tripp must notice my shocked expression and leans into me. "Who's that?"

I swallow hard, staring wide-eyed at Ayden's mother. "Mrs. Carson."

"I go by my maiden name now. You can call me Ms. Reynolds."

"Of course." I bite out a smile of unease. "What can I help you with?"

Ayden cashed her half-a-million-dollar check and spent it to buy land and build our home. If she suddenly wants it back, we don't have it.

"Well, for starters, I'd like to meet my granddaughter. And see my son."

Bonus Epilogue

Serena

EIGHT MONTHS LATER

"Are you excited to meet your little brother?" Mimi asks, holding my hand as we walk down the cold hallway of the hospital. Nana and Meemaw flew up from Texas a few days ago when Mom started having contractions and stayed here while she was in labor. Though I begged to stay, Dad had his mother pick me up and stay at her house until it was time to come.

"Yep! I wanna hold him first!" I smile wide. We've been preparing his nursery for months. I can't wait to hold him in the rocking chair I picked out.

Mimi laughs at my eagerness and shoots me a wink. She moved here after Christmas last year. It was cool finding out I had another grandparent. She dresses super fancy and lets me pick out expensive clothes and accessories when she takes me shopping. Mom tells me I shouldn't go overboard, but Mimi insists. I'm her only grandchild, and she spent years not knowing me—her words, not mine—so who I am to deny a grandma spoiling their granddaughter?

She's just as excited as I am for the new baby. My parents announced the news at Thanksgiving when everyone came to visit, and that's when Mimi asked Daddy if it was okay for her to move closer to us. She wasn't in his life and wanted a second chance. I was happy when he said she could.

Nana and Meemaw still live in Beaumont, but they come to visit a lot. I was excited to show them my new horse, Frankie. He's a quarter horse, and Noah's been teaching me how to ride him. When I'm older, I want to learn how to do tricks like Noah does on Donut. Mom said *no way*, but Dad said *we'll see*.

"Hey, sweetie," Dad greets when he opens the door to Mom's room. He pulls me in for a hug, then kisses Mimi on the cheek. "He's asleep, so we gotta stay quiet."

I tiptoe into the room and narrow my eyes on the little bundle wrapped in a blanket on Mom's lap. He's wearing a cute little blue hat, but when I get closer, I realize just how small he is.

"Come here, baby," Mom whispers, wrapping her arm around me. It'd been Mom and me for so long, and now over a year later, I have a dad and a new brother. It still feels crazy after all this time, but now I can't imagine life any other way. Moving here has been exciting and new. Mallory and Noah are the big sisters I never had. Dena and Garrett are another set of grandparents to spoil me, especially with Gramma's baking addiction.

I love it here.

"He looks so squishy," I say, staring at his pudgy cheeks.

Mom and Dad chuckle as Mimi stands behind me.

"Looks just like your father when he was born," she says.

179

"Are you ready to hold him?" Mom asks.

I beam. "Yes!"

Mom hands me a pillow, and then I settle into the chair. Dad carries him over and helps me hold his head. Looking down at him, I smile and brush my finger along his soft skin.

"Well, do we have a name?" Mimi asks.

During a gender reveal party a few months ago, we learned he was a boy, which was already exciting enough, but then they said I got to pick out his name. I took that job very seriously, but there was only one boy name I wanted.

I revealed it to my parents a while ago, but we haven't shared it with anyone else yet.

"You wanna tell her?" Dad asks.

I smile down at him, hoping he likes it too. "Howie Adam."

"It's perfect," Mimi says with tenderness in her voice. "Howie was a wonderful man."

While I'm named after Mimi's mom—Dad's grandmother, Serena Mae—I wanted Howie to have a name that was special to all of us. And when he's older, I'll tell him all about Uncle Howie, who looked over Mom and me when the explosion happened.

After an hour of holding him, he gets fussy and needs to eat. Mimi suggests we come back tomorrow with the rest of the Hollises, so I give them hugs and kisses and say goodbye.

Just as Mimi and I are walking toward the exit, we see Fisher rushing into the emergency room entrance with someone in his arms. He's the ranch's new farrier. Mallory told me he's also Noah's ex-boyfriend's dad. He's been around all summer and is nice but mostly quiet.

"Who's he carryin'?" I ask Mimi as we follow.

"I think Noah."

My heart races as I watch Fisher speak to a nurse, and then they bring a stretcher around, and that's when I see her face.

"Noah!" I shout, running toward them. Mimi yells for me to slow down, but I can't.

Fisher's eyes widen when he spots us, and Noah yelps in pain when he lays her down on it.

"What happened? Are you okay?" I ask as more nurses come out.

Noah winces with each breath she takes. I want to hold her hand and beg her to be okay. A man in dark scrubs starts listening to her heartbeat and asking her questions about pain.

"She fell off Donut," Fisher tells me. "She was doin' stunts, and I-I don't know. He got spooked right as she was doin' a flip, and he kicked and..." He's white as a ghost as he tries to recollect what happened. "I was supposed to be spottin' her, but it happened so fast. Next thing I knew, she was on the ground, not moving."

"Is she gonna be okay?"

He swallows hard. "God, I hope so. She has to be."

Fisher follows her when they roll Noah to the back. Mimi and I stay, making phone calls to the Hollises, and soon Daddy comes down too. He gives me a tight hug and reassures me Noah's going to be okay.

"Fisher looked like he was gonna have a heart attack," I tell him, worried for both of them.

Mimi leans in as if not to disturb the others around us. "I think Fisher likes her."

"Of course he does. We all like Noah," I tell her.

Daddy chuckles. "She means *likes* likes her. But are you sure, Ma? He's twice her age."

Mimi shrugs with a knowing grin. "Let's just say, I have a gut feelin'."

I want to ask what that means, but I'm too distracted by worrying about her. No one's given us an update, and I'm getting antsy. Daddy goes back upstairs to Mommy's room when Dena and Garrett show up. They give me hugs and tell me to go home and rest. They promise to give me an update as soon as they have one.

As Mimi drives, I bring up the conversation from before.

"What's it mean when a man *likes* likes a woman?"

"Well...it means you like them more than a friend."

"Like boyfriend girlfriend?" I furrow my brow.

"Yeah, like that."

"Fisher's too quiet. He's always staring at her but never says much. He almost looks at her like he's mad at her, so I don't think they're boyfriend girlfriend."

Mimi smirks, reaches over, and then pats my leg. "In that case, I think he's in *love* with her. Brooding men always look like that."

"What?" That makes *no* sense.

"You'll understand someday, sweetheart. When you're older and find a man you're not supposed to want or vice versa. Sometimes it's easier to hate them than it is to admit you love them."

I'm still confused by the time we get to Mimi's house. She lives in town, so it doesn't take long to get there. Since I'm ten now, I have my own phone and can text, so I send Noah a message, hoping she'll have her cell with her.

SERENA

> Please be okay, Noah. I haven't heard anything yet, and I'm getting scared.

I pace around the house until Mimi tells me it's time to get ready for bed. When I ask if she's gotten an update yet, she frowns. Mom sends me pictures of Howie, which cheers me up, but I hate that no one knows about Noah.

When I wake up the next day, the sun's already up, and I rush to check my phone. I squeal when I see Noah's name on the screen.

NOAH

> Hey kiddo. I'm home now. Call me when you wake up.

I nearly burst into tears as relief washes over me knowing my best friend is okay. After I use the bathroom, I FaceTime Noah.

"Hi, sweetie," she answers, her voice low and scratchy.

"Noah, what happened?" I immediately ask, noticing how tired and weak she looks.

I listen as she tells the story about how she fractured her ankle and broke three ribs doing a new trick move on Donut when he got spooked by a snake. Her foot got caught in the saddle strap and he dragged her. When she finally got loose, he reared and one of his hooves landed on her side. A potential client wants her to train a horse for trick shows, but Noah was trying it out on her own first before she agreed to it. Since Dena has a rule that she needed a spotter when she practices, Fisher was there to watch her.

"Will you still be able to come to the wedding?"

She's supposed to be in Mom and Dad's wedding party with me at the end of next month. We've been planning it for weeks. Even though my parents eloped at the courthouse, they're doing a vows ceremony and reception like Uncle Howie did.

"I hope so, but we'll have to wait and see. The doctor said it could take six-to-eight weeks to fully recover."

My jaw drops. "You're gonna be off that long? What about the horses?"

"Tripp's gonna have to take over, and your daddy will have to reschedule any that haven't come yet."

We continue talking a bit longer before I remember what else I wanted to ask her.

"Mimi says Fisher loves you. Is that true?"

She blinks. Licking her lips, she glances at something off-screen as if she's not alone but then brings her gaze back to the phone.

"No, sweetie. Why would she think that?"

I shrug. "She said she could just tell. Something in the way he looks at you."

Noah's cheeks go red, and I wonder if she's too hot. "I'm gonna get some rest now, but I'll text you later, okay?"

Smiling wide, I nod. "Okay! I'm gonna visit baby Howie soon. Then I'll have Mimi bring me over."

Noah grins and tells me that's fine, then we hang up.

After I eat breakfast and get dressed, Mimi and I drive to the hospital.

"So did you speak to Noah?"

"Yep!" I tell her all about our conversation, including her response about Fisher.

"Is that so?" Mimi's amused voice echoes through the car. "Ah...to be young and in love and lyin' about it."

I giggle at the way she singsongs the words.

I don't know if Noah's not telling me the truth, but I'm going to find out.

Come With Me

Curious about Noah and Fisher?
Find their story next in *Here With Me*

Keep reading for a sneak peek of chapter one.

Here With Me

A forbidden age gap stand-alone from small town romance author Brooke Montgomery about a daring horse trainer and her off-limits ex-boyfriend's dad...

When we met at the rodeo, I only knew his first name.

Sparks ignited between us, and we spent an unforgettable night together.
It's not until the morning after when I recognize his last name do I realize who he is.

So I do what any rational woman would and make the walk of shame while he sleeps. It's not like I'll ever see him again or have to explain why I left.

But I'm proven wrong when he shows up at my family's ranch as the new farrier.

We can't be more than friends—for many reasons.

Here With Me

He's twice my age, workplace relationships are off-limits, and he moved back to rebuild a relationship with his son—the one I used to date.

Getting involved would ruin everything.

As we struggle between right and wrong, our connection deepens even though his traumatic past makes him doubt he deserves a second chance.

But it doesn't matter when everything's against us, including a rival who's out to get me and my ex who's determined to win me back.

After a riding trick goes wrong on his watch, he insists on taking care of me. Even though the odds are stacked against us, we keep the truth to ourselves.

But secrets don't stay hidden for long in a Southern small town.

Scroll to read chapter one now!

Chapter One
Noah

"Goddamn, I love me some cowboys in tight Wranglers. 'Tis the rodeo season for fine asses," my childhood best friend, Magnolia, blurts way too loudly. A woman ahead of us glances over her shoulder with a scowl.

I burst out laughing, nudging my elbow into Magnolia's side as we walk into the arena. Not that her big mouth should even surprise me.

"Me too," my little cousin singsongs next to me.

"Mallory, shush your mouth. You're too young to be lookin'," I tell her.

"I'm twelve!"

"Exactly. Close your eyes." I attempt to cover them for her, but she shoves me away.

Magnolia snickers as we make our way up the ramp and into the arena. It smells like leather, dirt, and sweat. People in cowboy hats and boots walk around looking for a place to sit. The Franklin Rodeo is the heart of Southern rodeo in Tennessee. Every June, my family and I make the four-hour drive to watch the shows, eat lots of food, and listen to the live bands.

As a professional horse trainer on my family's ranch, I work with many clients for events like these. Barrel racing is one of my favorites to watch because I love that adrenaline high while anticipating them making it around the barrels without knocking them over. The excitement of each horse crossing the finish line gets me fired up every time.

One of my clients, Ellie, competes today. I've had butterflies in my stomach for the past week waiting for this. I live for the satisfaction of witnessing how the time I put in pays off. I also love showing my support when I can. I've worked with Ellie and her quarter horse for the past year, though she's been doing it a lot longer than that.

As we walk through to find a place to sit, I notice a few trainers glare at me and whisper to each other. I'm not surprised, considering it happens each time I'm at a competition, but it doesn't hurt any less. Most of them are in their forties and think I'm too young to have the success I do. I hear the rumors about how I only got here because of my last name and parents' money. On top of my being too young, the male trainers don't think I'm strong enough to train difficult breeds and like to degrade my skills to "good enough for a girl." But the truth is, I wouldn't keep my clients or get new ones if I couldn't back up my promises with talent.

"Don't look at them." Magnolia nudges me. "They're envious pricks with small dicks."

I snort, avert my gaze, and stay focused on maneuvering around people.

"And that's why they didn't get an invite to the Hollis fundraiser event of the decade," I gloat with a snarky smirk.

Chapter One

"Damn right. They could only wish to be good enough to be personally invited by *the* Noah Hollis."

I've been a trainer for years, but I've had to work at it every day since I was a teenager. My parents' money and ranch for me to practice on helped advance my skill, but my drive to learn and improve brought me to this level. Still, that makes me unlikable in this professional industry.

Six months ago, I proposed an idea to host a fundraising competition that'd benefit injured or rescued horses. I invited local trainers to bring their best clients to change the public's misperceptions of me and give them a chance to know the real me. Not only is it beneficial to the charity and community but it's a way for us to network as professionals.

My family's been all hands on deck in securing everything we need for it, and the first annual event will take place on our ranch in only a few weeks.

When we find seats, Mallory spots some friends she met at camp and asks to sit by them a few rows over.

"Don't leave the buildin' without me," I remind her before she wanders off. She's still close, so I can keep an eye on her. She moved in with my family a couple of years ago after my aunt and uncle passed away and has become a little sister to me. Although she drives me nuts sometimes, I'm super protective of her.

My parents and four older brothers are here somewhere. We venture off to different things, and since we brought three campers to sleep in, we come and go as we please. As an honorary family member, Magnolia tags along to most of our outings.

After ten minutes of waiting, the emcee announces Ellie's division.

"I'm gonna get closer."

Chapter One

"Well, shit. Don't leave me here." Magnolia follows me down the steps. You're not supposed to stand in the front and block others' views, but I'll only be a few minutes.

A few riders run, and one barrel tips over, making us wait for them to reset it.

"A hot guy in the row above ours is checkin' you out," Magnolia whispers.

Turning slightly, I see the man she's talking about. Shoulder-length brown hair. Sharp jawline covered in dark scruff and a matching mustache the perfect length for inner thigh scratching. His biceps look like they'll rip through his rolled-up shirtsleeves if he moves another inch.

My eyes widen as I return my gaze to Magnolia's smug expression.

"Told ya. He's bangin'."

That's an understatement.

I shrug so I don't give away how my heart pounds with how attractive and out of my league he is. "He looks too old."

More like twice my age.

At twenty-two, the oldest man I've dated was Jase Underwood, and he's only two years older than me.

"So what? You don't have to have Daddy issues to sample a finer cuisine."

I roll my eyes at her choice of words. Sneaking another glance, I notice his gaze remains fixated on me. He's rugged like a cowboy, which isn't much of a surprise at a place like this.

"He's probably glarin' at me for blockin' his view."

"No, babe. You *are* his view. That's a look of lust, trust me." She flips her long dark hair and steals another look.

"You would know that look, wouldn't ya?" I snort.

"The look of thinkin' dirty things. I bet he's undressed you in his mind three times and envisioned your boots wrapped around his neck."

I roll my eyes. "Doubtful. Wouldn't be surprised if he came down here and scolded me."

"Maybe he'll punish you with spankings..." She waggles her brow, and we get lost in a fit of giggles.

Clinging to the railing, I keep my attention ahead so I don't miss Ellie's entrance now that they've restarted.

Finally, Ellie and Ranger race into the arena. She's decked out in sparkly pink, including her cowboy hat, which I helped pick. She's not dubbed the Rodeo Princess for nothing.

"Yeah! Go, Ellie!" I cup my mouth and scream as she clears the first barrel.

Leaning as far over the railing as possible, I shout louder.

"Want me to lift ya up so you can be in there with her?" Magnolia mocks.

"Too bad I didn't make a sign."

She laughs but eventually gets into the spirit and cheers with me.

Ellie's posture is perfect as she rounds the second barrel and rushes for the third.

"C'mon, Ranger! Go, go, go!" I jump up and down at how flawlessly she's performing.

When Ellie rounds the final barrel, I nearly lose my mind. They race toward the finish line, and everyone goes wild.

"Fifteen point seven six eight," the emcee announces, then repeats it over the crowd.

"Holy shit!" I cover my mouth after I realize how loud I am.

"That should put her in first place, no problem," Magnolia points out.

"Her fastest barely cleared fifteen point nine. I can't believe how much time she shaved off."

Chapter One

"Probably all that cheerin' ya did. Encouraged them even more." She nudges me with a cheeky grin.

"Ha ha. But I bet you're right. Maybe I should add that into my trainin'. Sideline of me screamin' at you." I cackle.

"Speakin' of *screamin'*. Go celebrate by talkin' to the sexy cowboy. Maybe he'll have you screamin' later for a different reason." Magnolia pushes me toward the stairs, and if I weren't living on this adrenaline high, I'd run in the other direction.

I don't mind taking risks. In fact, I thrive off the excitement of trying new things. But when it comes to dating and guys in general, I say things that get me in trouble.

"Good thing I'm wearin' my lucky cowboy boots." And my favorite white floral sundress that makes my boobs look awesome. It's the beginning of summer, and the temp is already in the low eighties, so I wasn't about to sweat my ass off being outside most of the day.

Magnolia smirks and urges me to go.

I walk up to his row, excuse myself as I shift my body in front of a few people, then sit next to him.

"Hi." I angle my body toward him as he takes a swig of his Budweiser.

He chokes when he realizes I'm speaking to him.

"Hi," he coughs out.

"You don't mind if I sit here, do ya? I saw you kept lookin' at me and thought maybe I was in your way." I flash him a mischievous smile, then pretend to look in the same direction as I was standing. Tilting my head to where I stood, I add, "But now that I'm here, I don't see how I coulda blocked your view."

I return my gaze to his as a half smirk forms across his face. "No, I could see just fine."

His deep timbre has a shiver rippling down my spine. I'm eager to hear it again.

"Oh, good. So you musta been glarin' at me for another reason." Our knees are almost touching, and I'm tempted to inch closer until they do.

He stares at me as if he's contemplating his words. "I wasn't glarin'."

"Coulda fooled me. You were definitely starin' awfully hard, then." I lick my lips and wait for him to elaborate on why he fixated on me. When the awkward silence drags on, I continue, "Anyway...since you seem as comfortable as a cat in cold water with me sittin' here, I'll go back to my friend. You're free to join me. The view is great."

"Not as great as mine was."

I stare at him—half shocked and half giddy at his words. "A-are you hittin' on me?"

"Maybe I am."

Crossing my legs, I wave him on. "Well then, just go on and ask me."

He tilts his head as wrinkles form between his brows. "Ask you what?"

"For my number."

"I don't even know your name."

"It's Noah. What's yours?"

"Fisher."

"I like that. So now that we know each other, do you want my number or not?"

He brings his bottle back to his tempting lips and watches me over the neck while he takes a sip. "You're very blunt."

"And why shouldn't I be?" I ask, keeping our gazes locked. "Are you used to shy women? Is that what you prefer? If I'm not your type, you can just say so. It won't hurt my feelings."

"That's not it."

I shrug and say, "Okay," as if his lack of eagerness didn't

bruise my ego. "If you change your mind, I'm bartendin' at the Cantina lounge tonight. First beer's on me."

I've been a volunteer for the past few years since my family's ranch is a sponsor. My brothers pitch in too, but they don't do it for the charity proceeds. They're only after single girls' numbers, which is exactly why they'll need a babysitter at the fundraiser.

Before Fisher can respond, I sashay myself out of his row and back toward Magnolia.

Her eyes are wide, and her mouth is agape. "Where the hell did that side of you just come from?"

I link my arm through hers as I lead us to where Mallory sits.

"I channeled my inner Magnolia. Figured I'd never see him again anyway, so why'd it matter if I make a fool outta myself?"

"Jesus. By the way your bodies were leanin' into each other and the intense eye contact, y'all were turnin' me on for a minute." She makes a show of fanning herself.

We laugh as we take our seats in front of my little cousin, who's busy gossiping with her friend. I resist the urge to glance up to see if he's looking at me again but decide to play it cool as if I don't care either way. So much for going up there and giving him my number. Instead, I'm kicking myself and panicking about what a fool I am. Now I wish the ground would open up and save me from the humiliation.

Once all the racers have run, Ellie's declared the winner, and we shoot to our feet, clapping and letting out piercing whistles. I couldn't be more proud of her focus and determination. Even when she had bad training days, she'd get back up and work harder.

"Isn't that Craig Sanders?" Magnolia whispers in my ear as we watch the team roping event.

My eyes follow as she points in his direction, and my lip curls. "Unfortunately."

I'm not surprised to see him here as a trainer himself, but he's local to Sugarland Creek. He's probably trying to find clients or steal them from others.

He's a snake like that.

"Oh shit, he's comin' over." My back stiffens as he makes a beeline for us.

"Howdy." He tips his hat, and I cringe. "Congrats on the win."

"Thanks," I say. Although it's Ellie's win, he's bitter she went to me after she fired him last year.

"She was a little slow on that second barrel. Might wanna help her fix that so she doesn't have such a narrow win next time. Would hate to see her slip into second."

Magnolia shoots him a murderous glare as I force a grin. "I'll keep that in mind. Thanks so much for your valuable input."

His jaw twitches as if it's full of tobacco chew. Gross.

Mallory's clueless about what's happening and chimes in, "Which racer was yours?"

Magnolia stifles a laugh as I bite back a smile.

"Mine isn't here," he tells her in a forced drawl.

Craig can't keep clients because he has a shitty attitude and no patience.

"How come?" Mallory asks, ignorant of the irritation covering Craig's face.

Instead of answering, he gives me a nod. "See ya 'round, Noah."

"God, I hope not," I mutter.

He's another one who thinks he should be more successful

than me because he's older. He also blames me when his clients leave and hire me instead.

Once the events are over for the evening, Magnolia takes Mallory to our camper while I head to the lounge for my shift. She promises to stop in later, but considering my brother Tripp is here, I doubt she will.

She's crushed on him since middle school, but he's never returned the feelings or been the settling-down type. He's only two years older than me, so I can't blame him. Eventually, though, she'll move on from her crush, and he'll be too late.

As I hand out drinks and chat with customers, my mind wanders to Fisher. Every time someone approaches, my heart skips a beat at the thought of it being him. I'm not sure he'll show up, but I want to be ready if he does. I grab a napkin and write down my number. This way, if he chickens out and doesn't ask me, I'll just casually hand it to him. He can decide whether he wants to use it.

Grabbing another napkin, an idea hits, and I jot down my ex's number. If he asks for it and the vibes are off, I'll give him Jase's instead, and he'll be none the wiser.

About the Author

Brooke has been writing romance since 2013 under the *USA Today* Bestselling author pen names: Brooke Cumberland and Kennedy Fox, and now, **Brooke Montgomery** and **Brooke Fox**. She loves writing small town romance with big families and happily ever afters! She lives in the frozen tundra of Packer Nation with her husband, wild teenager, and four dogs. Brooke's addicted to iced coffee, leggings, and naps. She found her passion for telling stories during winter break one year in grad school—and she hasn't stopped since.

Find her on her website at
www.brookewritesromance.com
and follow her on social media:

facebook.com/brookemontgomeryauthor

instagram.com/brookewritesromance

amazon.com/author/brookemontgomery

tiktok.com/@brookewritesromance

goodreads.com/brookemontgomery

bookbub.com/authors/brooke-montgomery

threads.net/@brookewritesromance

bsky.app/profile/brookemontgomery.bsky.social

Made in United States
Troutdale, OR
05/14/2025

31338519R00125

Sugarland Creek series
Reading Order

Come With Me (Prequel)
Here With Me (#1)
Stay With Me (#2)
Fall With Me (#3)
Only With Me (#4)
Sin With Me (#5)

Each book can be read as a stand-alone and ends in a happily ever after. However, for the best reading experience, read in order.